Culinary Arts Institute®

WOK
FONDUE
& CHAFING DISH
COOKBOOK

Featured in cover photo:
a. Fondue Bourguignonne, 26
b. Stir-Fried Shrimp and Vegetables, 59
c. Glazed Whole Oranges, 78

WOK, FONDUE, AND CHAFING DISH COOKBOOK

The Culinary Arts Institute Staff:

Helen Geist: Director
Sherrill Weary: Editor
Helen Lehman: Assistant Editor
Edward Finnegan: Executive Editor
Charles Bozett: Art Director
Ethel La Roche: Editorial Assistant
Ivanka Simitic: Recipe Tester
Malinda Miller: Copy Editor
John Mahalek: Art Assembly

Book designed and coordinated
   by Charles Bozett

Illustrations by Laura Lee Lizak

Photographs by Bob Scott Studios

Adventures in Cooking SERIES

WOK
FONDUE
& CHAFING DISH
COOKBOOK

Culinary Arts Institute®

A DIVISION OF DELAIR PUBLISHING COMPANY, INC.

CONTENTS

Copyright © 1982, 1980 by
Delair Publishing Company Inc.
420 Lexington Avenue
New York, New York 10170

All rights reserved under the International and Pan-American Copyright Conventions. Manufactured in the United States of America and published simultaneously in Canada.

Library of Congress Catalog Card Number: 78-54620

ISBN: 0-8326-0605-7

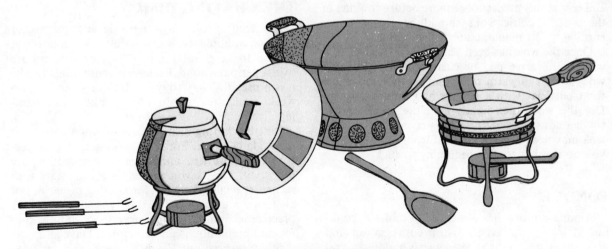

INTRODUCTION

Imagine serving your family an exotic vegetable dish cooked in a completely new way! Or think of how relaxed and intimate a party could be if your friends cooked their own main course. And what better way to show off your culinary skills than to prepare a flaming dessert, tableside, for that special occasion? The wok, fondue pot, and chafing dish can make entertaining both dramatic and fun. But they can add flair to everyday menus, too. Once you master the basics of their operation, you will be amazed at the variety of unique creations you can prepare, from appetizers and soups to desserts and beverages.

THE WOK

The wok is probably the oldest cooking utensil you could have in your kitchen. This cone-shaped pan was developed by the ancient Chinese to stir-fry foods. Stir-frying is frying foods such as vegetables and meats in hot oil while rapidly stirring and turning. Stir-fried meats cook quickly yet remain tender. Stir-fried vegetables also cook quickly, retaining their color and flavor well. Because stir-frying is an extremely fast cooking method, all ingredients must be prepared and ready to add before the cooking is started.

But wok cooking no longer necessarily means Chinese cooking. Modern cooks use the wok in place of their conventional skillet and saucepan for a variety of dishes. As a deep fryer the wok is an economical choice; its conical shape means it uses less oil. And, when fitted with a rack, it makes an excellent steamer. Bamboo racks are traditional, but you can improvise with a round cake rack.

To steam foods in a wok, place the rack above two to three inches of water. The rack should be positioned so that neither the rack nor food will touch the boiling water. Bring the water to a rapid boil. Place the food to be steamed in a shallow heat-proof dish or plate and place on the rack, making sure the water continues boiling rapidly.

A well-balanced wok with handles on both sides makes range-top cooking easier. The metal ring which comes with your wok is used to hold it in place on the burner. If yours is a gas range, the metal ring is used for all cooking except stir-frying. Center the wide end of the ring over the gas burner and place the wok on the narrow end. For stir-frying, remove the metal grate on the burner, and place the wok directly on the gas heating unit. This allows the flames to encircle the sides of the wok and enables you to cook as the Chinese actually do. For an electric range, specially made flat-bottom woks are available. These special woks can be put directly on the coils of the electric burner to get the high heat necessary for stir-frying. A regular wok can also be used on an electric range by placing the metal ring with its narrow end over the burner and the wide end up, holding the wok. The newer electric woks allow tableside cooking with all the benefits of the original wok.

"Seasoning" is a process used to keep food from sticking to the sides of the wok. A well-seasoned pan uses less oil in cooking. To season your wok, first wash it thoroughly and dry it well. Then, place it over a high heat. As the wok gets hot, add ¼ cup of cooking oil. Tilt the wok to coat the sides with oil. When the oil starts to smoke, remove the wok from the heat and let it cool. Wipe out the excess oil and repeat this process once more before cooking in the wok. Electric woks should be seasoned according to the manufacturer's instructions.

Once the wok has been seasoned, do not scrub it with an abrasive pad or cleanser. To clean your wok, soak it in warm water and gently remove any food particles with a sponge and mild detergent. Dry the wok, then lightly coat the inside with a small amount of cooking oil to prevent rusting. The wok may need to be reseasoned from time to time if you notice that food is beginning to stick.

FONDUE

Fondue is more than a method of tabletop cooking; it is a social event. Warm conversation and good times are a natural when guests huddle around a simmering fondue, and what could be easier on the hostess than to let her guests do their own cooking? A fondue party is fun to plan and easy to prepare. Let your creativity flow with the foods you choose as "dunkers" — perhaps mushrooms in a cheese fondue or banana chunks for a classic chocolate fondue. A fondue is sure to bring a festive mood to your gathering, whether served as an appetizer, main course, dessert, or all three.

Fondue pots come in all shapes and materials. There are metal pots, earthenware pots, pots with enameled or nonstick interiors, and even electric fondue pots. Also, a chafing dish can double as a fondue pot. Because of the high temperatures the oil is heated to in oil fondues, these must be cooked in a metal pot. Fondues can be brought to serving temperature on top of the range, and then transferred to a heat source to complete cooking at the table. As a heat source, alcohol burners or canned heat burners can be used if you do not have an electric fondue pot. But no matter what kind of heat source you choose, no more than four people should share an oil fondue or the oil will not stay hot enough to properly cook the meat.

THE CHAFING DISH

The chafing dish is a versatile and convenient piece of equipment for entertaining. On a buffet it is used to keep hot foods at serving temperature over a period of time. Because it gently heats foods, it is a practical way to warm leftovers. And it also works well when serving those sophisticated flaming dishes.

But the chafing dish is most commonly used for tableside cooking. For a flawless and elegant performance, practice and advance preparation are necessary. Unless you are experienced, start with recipes specially designed for chafing dishes as not all foods are suitable for this type of cooking. A practice session to familiarize yourself with the timing and preparation can be helpful. Have all ingredients measured out, ready to cook, and arranged attractively before starting. If you follow these practices, you will be assured of success every time.

Though the chafing dish is dramatic, it is also portable, quick, and easy to use. The basic chafing dish consists of a stand, a cooking pan, a water pan, a cover, and a burner. A removable water pan is a desired feature as it allows for direct cooking, such as sauteeing, required in some recipes. Otherwise, direct cooking must be done on top of the range. If slow, even heating is desired, the water pan is filled with ¼ inch boiling water and the cooking process is similar to cooking in a double boiler.

The most common sources of heat for chafing dishes are alcohol and canned heat, though some electric chafing dishes are available. These three types offer high enough heat to actually cook foods as well as keep them warm.

CULINARY ARTS INSTITUTE has assembled many traditional favorites as well as exciting new variations in this book. To help you get the most out of your wok, fondue pot, or chafing dish, there are recipes for every course of the meal. Each recipe has been kitchen-tested so that you can cook with confidence and expect to get compliments.

Cheese Fondue with Apples

1 can (11 ounces) condensed Cheddar cheese soup
2 packages (8 ounces each) cream cheese, softened and cut into pieces
1 cup dairy sour cream
½ teaspoon salt
½ teaspoon dry mustard
⅛ teaspoon garlic powder
½ teaspoon Worcestershire sauce
2 drops Tabasco
¼ cup sherry
4 or 5 apples
Lemon juice for dipping apple slices

1. In a fondue pot or chafing dish, combine soup with cream cheese, blending well.
2. Add remaining ingredients, except apples; mix well. Cook over low heat, stirring occasionally, until cheese melts and mixture is smooth.
3. Meanwhile, slice apples and dip in lemon juice.
4. Keep fondue warm while dipping apple slices.

About 4½ cups fondue

Hot Cheese Dunk

3 tablespoons butter or margarine
1 tablespoon flour
¼ teaspoon white pepper
¼ teaspoon Tabasco
½ cup instant nonfat dry milk solids
1 can (10½ ounces) chicken bouillon
½ medium onion
1 cup freshly grated Parmesan cheese
4 ounces Swiss cheese, shredded (about 1 cup)

1. In cooking pan of a chafing dish, melt butter. Blend in flour, pepper, and Tabasco.
2. Dissolve nonfat dry milk in bouillon. Gradually stir into flour mixture and add onion. Cook over medium heat, stirring constantly, until sauce thickens.
3. Remove onion and stir in cheeses until melted. Place over hot water to keep mixture warm.
4. Serve hot as a dunking sauce for cooked shrimp, ham cubes, rye toast, apple slices, or fresh uncooked vegetables.

About 2 cups dunk

Note: Dunk thickens upon standing and may be thinned with small amounts of chicken bouillon.

Cheesy Tuna-Onion Fondue

2 cans (6½ or 7 ounces each) tuna
1 pound pasteurized process American cheese, shredded (about 4 cups)
1 cup milk
3 tablespoons chopped parsley
1 tablespoon instant minced onion
Unsalted crackers
Corn chips
Potato chips

1. Drain tuna and flake, if desired.
2. Put shredded cheese into a saucepan and set over medium heat. Pour milk over the cheese. Stir until cheese is completely melted.
3. Mix in tuna, parsley, and onion. Heat thoroughly, stirring constantly.
4. Turn into a fondue saucepan and keep warm while serving with bowls of crackers, corn chips, and potato chips for dippers.

6 servings

Chili con Queso Dip

1 cup chopped onion
2 cans (4 ounces each) green
    chilies, chopped and drained
2 large cloves garlic, mashed
2 tablespoons cooking oil
1 pound process sharp Cheddar
    cheese, cut into chunks
1 teaspoon Worcestershire sauce
¼ teaspoon paprika
¼ teaspoon salt
½ cup tomato juice

1. Sauté onion, green chilies, and garlic in oil in cooking pan of chafing dish over medium heat until onion is tender.
2. Reduce heat to low, and add remaining ingredients, except tomato juice. Cook, stirring constantly, until cheese is melted.
3. Add tomato juice gradually until dip is the desired consistency. Place over hot water to keep warm.
4. Serve with **corn chips.**

3 ¼ cups dip

Hot Cheese Dunking Sauce

½ cup shredded Cheddar cheese
¾ cup milk
3 tablespoons condensed cream of
    mushroom soup
⅛ teaspoon pepper
1½ teaspoons Worcestershire sauce
2 tablespoons prepared horseradish
    French bread, cut into 1-inch
    cubes

1. In cooking pan of chafing dish or in fondue pot, combine cheese and milk. Place over low heat, add soup, and stir constantly until cheese is melted,
2. Stir in pepper, Worcestershire sauce, and horseradish.
3. Keep hot in chafing dish and serve with French bread cubes.

1½ cups sauce

Hot Crab Meat Dip

2 tablespoons butter or
    margarine
3 tablespoons flour
½ teaspoon salt
1 cup milk
¼ cup shredded Cheddar
    cheese
½ cup mayonnaise
2 tablespoons tomato paste
¼ teaspoon Worcestershire
    sauce
1 cup flaked crab meat

1. Melt butter in cooking pan of chafing dish. Stir in flour and salt. Add milk, stirring until mixture thickens. Blend in cheese.
2. Combine mayonnaise, tomato paste, and Worcestershire sauce. Stir in some of the hot mixture. Pour back into cooking pan. Stir in crab meat.
3. Keep warm while serving with **crackers, toast rounds, potato chips,** or **corn chips.**

About 1½ cups dip

Hot Curry Dip

¼ cup butter or margarine
¼ cup finely chopped onion
2 tablespoons flour
3 tablespoons chopped crystallized
   ginger
2 tablespoons curry powder
2 teaspoons salt
1 teaspoon sugar
¼ teaspoon crushed dried mint
   leaves
4 whole cloves
   Few grains cayenne pepper
2 cups milk
½ cup (2 ounces) moist shredded
   coconut
½ cup lime juice
½ cup whipping cream

1. In cooking pan of chafing dish, melt butter over medium heat. Add onion and cook until transparent, stirring occasionally. Blend in flour and heat until the mixture bubbles.
2. Add ginger, curry powder, salt, sugar, mint leaves, cloves, and cayenne; mix well. Remove from heat and gradually stir in milk.
3. Cook rapidly, stirring constantly, over direct heat until sauce thickens. Place over simmering water and cover. Cook 30 minutes, stirring occasionally.
4. Stir in coconut, cover, and cook 10 minutes longer. Gradually stir in lime juice, then gradually add whipping cream, stirring constantly. Continue cooking until sauce is heated through.
5. Serve warm with **crisp raw vegetables** or **cooked shrimp.**

About 3½ cups sauce

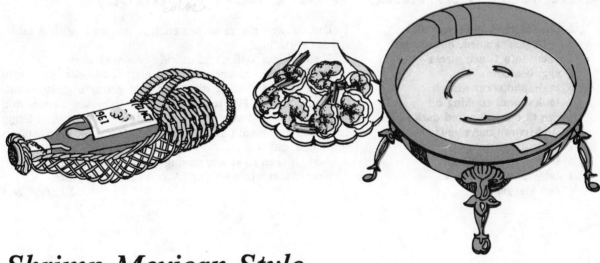

Shrimp Mexican Style

1 can (4 ounces) peeled green
   chilies
½ cup minced onion
3 medium cloves garlic, minced
¼ cup olive oil
2 tablespoons flour
1 cup half-and-half
8 ounces Monterey Jack cheese,
   shredded (about 2 cups)
4 ounces sharp Cheddar cheese,
   shredded (about 1 cup)
¼ cup dry white wine
½ teaspoon paprika
1 pound cooked shrimp, shelled,
   deveined, and cut in bite-size
   pieces

1. Rinse seeds from chilies; dice and set aside.
2. In cooking pan of chafing dish, sauté onion and garlic in oil over medium heat until soft but not browned. Add flour, stirring constantly. Stir over medium heat 3 minutes.
3. Gradually add half-and-half, stirring until very smooth. Add both cheeses gradually, stirring after each addition until the mixture is smooth.
4. Stir in wine, paprika, diced chilies, and shrimp. Heat thoroughly and place over simmering water to keep warm.
5. Serve warm with **corn chips**, pieces of **crisp fried tortillas**, or **crackers.**

4 to 6 servings

Tomato Bagna Cauda

1 can (8 ounces) tomato sauce
¼ cup cooking oil
1 tablespoon anchovy paste
1 clove garlic, crushed in a garlic
    press
⅛ teaspoon pepper
¼ teaspoon tarragon leaves
    Fresh mushrooms, broccoli and
    cauliflower flowerets, celery
    sticks, carrot sticks,
    zucchini strips

1. In a fondue pot or chafing dish, stir together all ingredients except fresh vegetables. Stir over low heat until smooth and thoroughly heated.
2. Keep hot and serve fresh vegetables as dunkers.

About 1¼ cups sauce

Chicken Tantalizers in Cherry Sauce

2 pounds chicken breasts and
    thighs, skinned, boned, and
    cut into 1-inch pieces
1 egg, beaten
6 tablespoons cornstarch
3 tablespoons cooking oil
1 can (8 ounces) pitted dark sweet
    cherries (undrained)
2 tablespoons sugar
1½ teaspoons cornstarch
1 tablespoon soy sauce
¼ cup vinegar

1. Dip chicken pieces in beaten egg, and coat with 6 tablespoons cornstarch.
2. Heat oil in a skillet and quickly brown chicken.
3. Purée undrained cherries in an electric blender, pour into cooking pan of chafing dish, and heat gently over low heat. Combine sugar, 1½ teaspoons cornstarch, soy sauce, and vinegar. Add gradually to cherry mixture while stirring. Bring to boiling over medium heat and boil 1 minute, or until sauce is thickened and clear.
4. Add chicken to sauce, mixing gently. Heat thoroughly.
5. Keep warm while serving. Accompany with picks.

50 appetizers

Oriental Chicken Wings

10 chicken wings
½ cup soy sauce
2 tablespoons sugar
1 tablespoon dry sherry
½ teaspoon anise seed
⅓ cup water

1. Cut tips off chicken wings and discard. Cut wings in two at joints. Wash in warm water and dry.
2. In a heavy saucepan, combine chicken wings and remaining ingredients. Bring to boiling, reduce heat, cover, and simmer 20 minutes; stir occasionally.
3. Remove cover and simmer another 15 minutes, basting frequently until about ½ cup liquid remains.
4. Turn into cooking pan of a chafing dish, spoon liquid over wings, and serve while hot.

20 appetizers

Note: If desired, the prepared chicken wings may be refrigerated in the sauce overnight for a stronger flavor and reheated in chafing dish before serving.

Saucy Cocktail Franks

1 jar (10 ounces) currant jelly
⅓ cup prepared mustard
1 pound frankfurters, cut diagonally into 1-inch pieces

1. In cooking pan of a chafing dish, melt jelly and blend in mustard; heat thoroughly.
2. Stir in frankfurters, coating each piece; heat thoroughly, stirring occasionally.
3. Serve with picks.

8 to 12 servings

Teriyaki

1 teaspoon ground ginger
⅓ cup soy sauce
¼ cup honey
1 clove garlic, minced
1 teaspoon grated onion
1 pound beef sirloin tip, cut into 2x½x¼-inch strips
2 to 3 tablespoons cooking oil
1 tablespoon cornstarch
½ cup water
⅛ teaspoon red food coloring

1. Blend ginger, soy sauce, honey, garlic, and onion in a bowl. Add meat; marinate about 1 hour.
2. Remove meat, reserving marinade, and brown quickly on all sides in the hot oil in a large wok. Remove meat from wok.
3. Stir a blend of cornstarch, water, and food coloring into the reserved marinade and pour into wok. Bring rapidly to boiling and cook 2 to 3 minutes, stirring constantly.
4. Add meat to thickened marinade to glaze; remove and drain on wire rack.
5. Insert a frilled wooden pick into each meat strip and serve with the thickened marinade.

About 24 appetizers

Swedish Meatballs

1 pound ground round steak
½ pound ground pork
½ cup prepared instant mashed potatoes
½ cup fine dry bread crumbs
1 egg, beaten
1 teaspoon salt
¼ teaspoon pepper
½ teaspoon brown sugar
¼ teaspoon allspice
¼ teaspoon nutmeg
⅛ teaspoon cloves
⅛ teaspoon ginger
½ cup fine dry bread crumbs
3 tablespoons butter or margarine

1. Lightly mix in a large bowl the ground meats, potatoes, ½ cup crumbs, egg, and a mixture of salt, pepper, brown sugar, allspice, nutmeg, cloves, and ginger.
2. Shape mixture lightly into ¾-inch balls. Roll balls in remaining crumbs.
3. Heat butter in cooking pan of chafing dish. Add the meatballs and brown on all sides; shake pan frequently to brown evenly and to keep balls round. Cook, covered, about 15 minutes, or until meatballs are thoroughly cooked.
4. Keep hot while serving.

About 4 dozen meatballs

Hot Spicy Meatballs

Sauce:
- ¾ cup ketchup
- ½ cup water
- ¼ cup cider vinegar
- 2 tablespoons brown sugar
- 1 tablespoon minced onion
- 2 teaspoons Worcestershire sauce
- 1½ teaspoons salt
- 1 teaspoon dry mustard
- ¼ teaspoon pepper
- 3 drops Tabasco
  Few grains cayenne pepper

Meatballs:
- ¾ pound ground beef
- ¾ cup fine dry bread crumbs
- 1½ tablespoons minced onion
- ½ teaspoon prepared horseradish
- 3 drops Tabasco
- 2 eggs, beaten
- ¾ teaspoon salt
- ½ teaspoon pepper
- 1 tablespoon butter or margarine

1. To make sauce, combine all sauce ingredients in a bowl. Set aside.
2. To make meatballs, mix together lightly the remaining ingredients except the butter. Shape mixture into balls about ¾ inch in diameter.
3. Melt butter in cooking pan of chafing dish. Add the meatballs and brown over direct heat, shaking pan frequently to produce even browning and keep balls round.
4. When meatballs are browned, pour off fat and pour sauce over meatballs. Cover and continue to cook about 10 minutes, shaking cooking pan occasionally.
5. Place over pan of simmering water to keep hot while serving. Spear with wooden picks.

About 3 dozen meatballs

Gourmet Meatballs

- ½ pound Braunschweiger
- 2 eggs, fork beaten
- ½ pound ground beef
- 1 cup fine dry bread crumbs
- ¼ cup ketchup
- ½ teaspoon salt
- ¼ cup butter or margarine
- 1 envelope (1½ ounces) dry onion soup mix
- 1½ cups hot water

1. Combine Braunschweiger and eggs. Add ground beef, bread crumbs, ketchup, and salt, mixing thoroughly. Chill about 1 hour. Shape into ¾-inch balls.
2. Melt butter in large skillet. Add meatballs and cook over medium heat until evenly browned, turning balls carefully.
3. Place meatballs in cooking pan of chafing dish. Stir soup mix into hot water and pour over meatballs. Cover pan and cook meatballs slowly 15 minutes.
4. Keep warm and serve with picks.

About 6 dozen meatballs

Shrimp Balls

- 3 cups finely chopped cooked shrimp
- 1½ cups finely rolled shredded wheat wafer crumbs
- 2 eggs, well beaten
- ¼ cup butter or margarine
- 1 clove garlic, finely minced

1. Combine shrimp, wafer crumbs, and eggs; mix well. Shape into small balls about ¾ inch in diameter.
2. Melt butter in cooking pan of chafing dish. Stir in garlic. Sauté shrimp balls in butter until lightly browned on all sides.
3. Serve hot with picks.

About 2½ dozen balls

Exotic Appetizer Balls

1 pound lean ground beef
1 egg, fork beaten
½ teaspoon Worcestershire sauce
8 drops Tabasco
1 tablespoon instant coffee
1 teaspoon salt
⅛ teaspoon pepper
4 teaspoons instant minced onion
    softened in 4 teaspoons water
½ to ¾ cup chopped water
    chestnuts
    Fine cracker crumbs
    Butter or margarine

1. Lightly mix meat with egg, Worcestershire sauce, and Tabasco. Blend with a mixture of coffee, salt, and pepper. Add the softened onion and water chestnuts; mix lightly.
2. Form mixture into 1-inch balls. Roll in crumbs.
3. Brown meatballs in hot butter in a large heavy skillet over medium heat; shake frequently to obtain even browning and round balls.
4. Turn into cooking pan of chafing dish, spear with wooden picks, and serve hot.

About 5½ dozen balls

Marinated Artichoke Hearts

1 package (10 ounces) frozen
    artichoke hearts or 2 cans (8
    ounces each) artichoke hearts
⅓ cup cooking oil
2 tablespoons tarragon-flavored
    white wine vinegar
1 clove garlic, crushed in a
    garlic press
½ teaspoon salt
¼ teaspoon pepper
⅛ teaspoon oregano
¼ teaspoon parsley flakes
    Dash Tabasco

1. Thaw frozen artichokes, or drain and rinse canned artichokes. If whole, slice vertically in half.
2. In cooking pan of a chafing dish, combine remaining ingredients. Add artichoke hearts and simmer in sauce on top of range until tender (about 8 minutes). If using canned artichoke hearts, add to sauce and just heat through.
3. Keep warm while serving.

About 2 dozen artichoke halves

Fried Oriental Shrimp Balls

2 pounds fresh uncooked shrimp
1 can (5 ounces) water chestnuts,
    drained and coarsely chopped
1 egg, slightly beaten
1 tablespoon cornstarch
¼ teaspoon sherry extract
½ teaspoon salt
    Oil for deep frying

Sauce:
1 tablespoon cornstarch
¼ teaspoon sugar
1 tablespoon soy sauce
¾ cup chicken bouillon

1. Wash, shell, devein, and finely chop shrimp. Combine with water chestnuts, egg, cornstarch, sherry extract, and salt. Form into balls about 1 inch in diameter.
2. Pour oil into a wok, filling it not more than a third full, but at least 1 inch deep. Heat oil to 375°F. Fry shrimp balls about 6 at a time until golden brown. Drain on paper towels and keep shrimp balls warm in a low oven, if necessary.
3. Combine ingredients for sauce in a small fondue pot. Cook over low heat until thickened, stirring constantly.
4. Keep the sauce warm and serve with hot shrimp balls.

About 4 dozen appetizers

Fried Shrimp with Dunking Sauce

2 pounds uncooked shrimp
Salt
2 eggs, slightly beaten
1 can (3 ounces) chow mein noodles, finely crushed
Oil for deep frying
Dunking Sauce or Zesty Sauce

1. Wash shrimp; remove shells (not tails) and black veins. Drain shrimp and sprinkle with salt.
2. Dip each shrimp into beaten egg and then into finely crushed chow mein noodles, coating well.
3. Pour oil into a wok, filling not more than a third full yet at least 1 inch deep. Heat to 375°F.
4. Drop shrimp, about 6 at a time, into hot oil. Fry, turning as necessary, until golden, and drain on absorbent paper.
5. Serve hot with desired sauce.

About 60 appetizers

Dunking Sauce: Add enough water to **2 tablespoons dry mustard** to make a smooth paste. Blend in **½ cup soy sauce.**

Zesty Sauce: Blend **1 tablespoon ground ginger, ¼ clove garlic** (crushed in a garlic press), **¼ cup water, 2 tablespoons sugar,** and **½ cup soy sauce.**

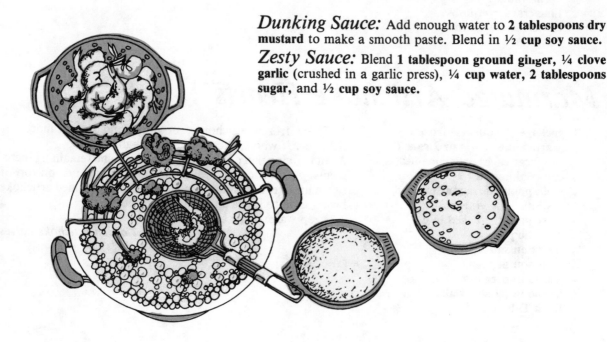

Brussels Sprouts with Dunking Sauce

2¼ cups chicken broth (dissolve 2 chicken bouillon cubes in 2¼ cups boiling water)
1 pound fresh Brussels sprouts (or two 10-ounce packages frozen Brussels sprouts)
2 tablespoons butter or margarine
1 tablespoon flour
1 teaspoon salt
½ teaspoon caraway seed
¼ teaspoon cayenne pepper
1 cup milk
1½ cups dairy sour cream

1. Heat broth in a saucepan until boiling. Add Brussels sprouts and boil, uncovered, 5 minutes. Cover and boil 5 to 10 minutes, or until just tender. (Cook frozen Brussels sprouts in the chicken broth following package directions.)
2. Meanwhile, heat butter in a fondue saucepan; stir in a mixture of flour, salt, caraway seed, and cayenne pepper. Heat until mixture bubbles. Add milk, cooking and stirring until mixture comes to boiling. Boil 1 to 2 minutes, stirring constantly.
3. Reduce heat and stir in sour cream. Heat thoroughly (do not boil). Keep sauce hot during serving.
4. Drain cooked Brussels sprouts and turn into a serving dish. Spear each sprout and dunk into the sauce.

About 8 servings

Carrot Nibblers

1 pound carrots
2 to 3 tablespoons cooking oil
2 large cloves garlic, minced
1 tablespoon chopped onion
¼ cup vinegar
1½ teaspoons salt
⅛ teaspoon pepper
½ teaspoon dry mustard
1 tablespoon whole pickling spices
1 onion, thinly sliced

1. Wash and pare carrots. Cut into 3x¼-inch strips, and set aside.
2. Heat oil in a large wok. Stir in garlic and onion and cook over low heat about 5 minutes. Stir in vinegar, salt, pepper, dry mustard, spices (tied in cheesecloth), and carrots.
3. Cook, covered, over low heat about 10 minutes, or until carrots are crisp-tender. Remove spice bag and turn carrots into a shallow dish. Top with sliced onion, cover, and refrigerate overnight.

8 servings

Cheese Balls

4 ounces Cheddar cheese, shredded
(about 1 cup)
1 teaspoon flour
¼ teaspoon salt
Dash pepper
1 egg white
Oil for deep frying

1. Mix cheese, flour, salt, and pepper.
2. Beat egg white to stiff, not dry, peaks. Fold beaten egg white into cheese mixture. Form into small balls, using a rounded tablespoon of the mixture for each.
3. Heat the oil to 365° F in a wok. Fry the cheese balls, a few at a time, until brown. Serve while warm.

12 cheese balls

Ham Nibbles

2 cups ground cooked ham
1 can (12 ounces) vacuum-packed
whole kernel corn, drained
2 cups cheese-cracker crumbs
¼ cup mayonnaise
2 eggs, well beaten
Oil for deep frying

1. Combine the ham, corn, 1 cup of the crumbs, mayonnaise, and eggs.
2. Shape mixture into ¾- to 1-inch balls. Roll in remaining crumbs. Set aside about 30 minutes.
3. Fill a large wok with oil not more than a third full, and heat to 375°F. Fry balls uncrowded in hot fat 2 minutes, or until browned. Remove to drain on absorbent paper.
4. Serve on a heated platter accompanied with picks.

About 7 dozen appetizers

Peanut Cocktail Fritters

½ cup boiling water
¼ cup peanut oil
¼ teaspoon salt
½ cup flour
2 eggs
1 cup finely chopped dry roasted
   peanuts
Peanut oil for deep frying
Salt

1. In a saucepan, combine water, ¼ cup peanut oil, and ¼ teaspoon salt. Bring to a full boil. Add flour all at once, and stir vigorously over low heat until mixture forms a ball and leaves sides of pan. Remove from heat.
2. Add eggs, one at a time, beating thoroughly after each is added. Stir in chopped peanuts, blending well. Form into 1-inch balls.
3. Heat oil to 365°F in a wok. Fry fritters, about 10 at a time, until golden brown (3 to 4 minutes).
4. Drain on paper towels, sprinkle with salt, and serve while hot.

5 dozen fritters

Beef Sub Gum Soup

½ pound beef round, cut into
   small cubes
1 tablespoon cooking oil
1 can (20 ounces) Chinese
   vegetables, drained
2 cans (10½ ounces each) condensed beef broth or bouillon
2 cups water
¼ cup uncooked rice
2 tablespoons soy sauce
¼ teaspoon monosodium glutamate
⅛ teaspoon pepper
1 egg, beaten

1. In a large wok, brown beef in hot oil. Chop vegetables and add to the browned meat with remaining ingredients, except egg.
2. Bring soup to boiling, stirring to blend. Cover and simmer 40 minutes.
3. Remove soup from heat and slowly stir in the egg. Let stand until egg is set.

About 6 servings

Chinese Chicken-Mushroom Soup

1 pound chicken breasts
½ teaspoon salt
1 tablespoon cooking oil
10 medium-size mushrooms, sliced
4 chicken bouillon cubes
4 cups hot water
1 tablespoon cornstarch
3 tablespoons cold water
1 tablespoon soy sauce
2 tablespoons lemon juice

1. Bone chicken breasts, remove skin, and cut into ¼-inch-wide strips, 1½ to 2 inches long. Sprinkle with salt and let stand 30 minutes.
2. Heat oil in a wok and sauté mushrooms a few minutes until golden. Remove from wok. Dissolve bouillon cubes in hot water and set aside.
3. Mix cornstarch with cold water. Stir in soy sauce. Combine with chicken bouillon in the wok. Bring to boiling, add chicken pieces, and simmer, covered, 5 minutes.
4. Add mushrooms and lemon juice to soup, adding more salt, if necessary. Heat gently without boiling.
5. Serve with a thin **lemon slice** in each bowl.

5 servings

Chili con Queso Dip, 8

Chinese Cabbage Soup

1 chicken breast (¾ pound),
    cooked
7 cups chicken broth
6 cups sliced Chinese cabbage
    (celery cabbage)
1 teaspoon soy sauce
1¼ teaspoons salt
¼ teaspoon pepper

1. Cut chicken into strips about ⅛ inch wide and 1½ to 2 inches long. Combine with chicken broth in a large wok and heat only until hot. Add Chinese cabbage and cook 3 to 4 minutes (only until cabbage is crisp-tender; do not overcook).
2. Stir in soy sauce, salt, and pepper. Serve hot.

6 servings

Note: If desired, romaine may be substituted for the cabbage. Reduce cooking time to 1 minute.

Oriental Soup

2 tablespoons cooking oil
2 cups diagonally sliced celery
½ cup chopped onion
1 can (16 ounces) bean sprouts,
    drained
1 can (5 ounces) water chestnuts,
    drained and chopped
2 quarts rich beef broth (made
    with bouillon cubes, if desired)
Salt and pepper to taste

1. In a large wok, heat oil and stir in celery and onion. Cook until crisp-tender, stirring frequently.
2. Stir in remaining ingredients and heat thoroughly.
3. Serve with crisp chow mein noodles sprinkled over individual bowls, if desired.

6 servings

Spanish Chicken Soup with Sausage

1 pound bulk pork sausage
1 teaspoon sage
1 teaspoon ground thyme
¼ teaspoon salt
½ cup finely chopped almonds
1 onion, cut into 8 wedges
1 large clove garlic, minced
1 can (10½ ounces) condensed
    chicken broth
1 can (10½ ounces) condensed
    cream of chicken soup
1 cup dry white wine
¼ cup dry sherry
¾ cup diced green pepper
1 bay leaf
⅛ teaspoon Tabasco
½ cup slivered almonds, toasted
    (see Note)
1 ounce (1 square) semisweet
    chocolate, shaved

1. Mix sausage with sage, ½ teaspoon thyme, salt, and the chopped almonds. Shape into balls about 1½ inches in diameter.
2. In a large wok, cook the meatballs over medium heat until evenly browned and thoroughly cooked. Remove meatballs from wok.
3. Stir in onion and garlic; sauté 5 minutes. Add chicken broth, condensed soup, wines, green pepper, bay leaf, Tabasco, and remaining thyme. Salt to taste.
4. Cover and simmer about 5 minutes, stirring occasionally. Uncover and simmer 10 minutes. Ladle into soup bowls and garnish with slivered almonds and shaved chocolate.

4 servings

Note: To toast almonds, spread in a shallow pan. Heat in a 350°F oven or on top of range, stirring occasionally, until almonds are lightly browned.

Chinese Chicken-Mushroom Soup, 16

Chicken-Vegetable Soup with Rice Dumplings

1 quart clear chicken stock
6 small white onions
1½ cups canned tomatoes
1 cup fresh uncooked peas
½ cup sliced celery
½ cup sliced carrots
⅔ cup frozen okra
6 tablespoons uncooked rice
1 tablespoon sugar
1½ teaspoons salt
¼ teaspoon pepper
Rice Dumplings

1. In a large wok, combine stock, vegetables, rice, and seasonings.
2. Bring to boiling; cover, reduce heat, and simmer 30 minutes, or until vegetables are tender.
3. Place dumplings on top of vegetables and cook as directed.

About 4 servings

Rice Dumplings

¾ cup flour
1 teaspoon baking powder
½ teaspoon salt
1½ tablespoons minced parsley
¼ cup milk
1½ teaspoons butter or margarine, melted
1 egg, beaten
½ cup cooked rice

1. Stir together flour, baking powder, salt, and parsley.
2. Stir milk and melted butter into beaten egg. Add to flour mixture and stir just enough to blend. Add rice and beat until blended.
3. Drop from tablespoon onto vegetables. (If spoon is dipped into hot stock and then into batter, dumplings will slide off easily.)
4. Cover and simmer 15 minutes. Do not lift cover during cooking time.

4 dumplings

Shrimp and Artichoke Potage

2 tablespoons butter or margarine
¼ cup chopped green onion
¼ teaspoon thyme, crushed
2 cans (10¾ ounces each) condensed tomato-rice soup
2 soup cans water
1 cup cooked artichoke hearts, cut into pieces
Seasoned salt
1 cup cooked shrimp, cut into pieces
2 teaspoons lemon juice

1. Heat butter in a large wok; add onion and thyme and cook about 5 minutes, stirring mixture occasionally.
2. Stir in condensed soup and water until well blended. Sprinkle the artichokes generously with the seasoned salt; add with the shrimp to the soup.
3. Heat thoroughly (do not boil). Remove from heat and stir in lemon juice. Serve hot.

6 servings

Tomato Cream

2 tablespoons butter
2 leeks, chopped (about 2½ cups)
2 carrots, diced (about 1 cup)
2 tablespoons flour
2½ cups beef broth
1 to 2 teaspoons sugar
¼ teaspoon salt
4 large ripe tomatoes (2 pounds), cut into pieces

1. Heat butter in a large wok. Add leeks and carrots; cook, stirring occasionally, until lightly browned. Stir in flour and heat until bubbly.
2. Blend in broth; bring to boiling, stirring constantly, and cook 3 minutes.
3. Stir in sugar, salt, and tomatoes; simmer, covered, 1 hour.
4. Force mixture through a coarse sieve or food mill. Serve while very hot.

4 servings

Vegetable Bouillon

1 can (10½ ounces) condensed beef broth
1 soup can water
1 can (6 ounces) cocktail vegetable juice
2 tablespoons finely chopped green pepper
3 radishes, finely chopped
½ teaspoon instant minced onion

1. Bring broth, water, and vegetable juice to boiling in a wok.
2. Add green pepper, radishes, and onion. Simmer, uncovered, 5 to 8 minutes.
3. Serve hot, garnished with **sprigs of parsley**.

4 servings

Almond Soup

1 cup blanched, toasted, and salted almonds (see Note)
1 cup water
4 egg yolks
3 chicken bouillon cubes
1 slice onion (¼ inch thick)
½ teaspoon sugar
2 cups water
1 cup half-and-half
Grated orange peel

1. Place almonds, 1 cup water, egg yolks, bouillon cubes, onion, and sugar in an electric blender container. Cover and blend until almonds are finely ground. Pour into a 2-quart chafing dish. Stir in 2 cups water.
2. Cook over low heat 10 to 15 minutes, or until thickened, stirring constantly; do not boil. Stir in half-and-half.
3. Serve immediately, garnished with grated orange peel.

5 or 6 servings

Note: To toast and salt almonds, place nuts in a shallow baking dish or pie pan. Brush lightly with butter, margarine, or cooking oil. Heat at 350°F until lightly browned, stirring occasionally. Sprinkle with salt.

CHEESE AND EGGS

Cheese Rabbit Fondue

1 small clove garlic
2 cups beer
1 pound sharp Cheddar cheese, shredded (about 4 cups)
3 tablespoons flour
1 teaspoon Worcestershire sauce
½ teaspoon dry mustard
2 tablespoons chopped chives or green onion top (optional)
1 loaf sourdough French bread, cut into 1-inch cubes

1. Rub inside of a nonmetal fondue pot with garlic; discard garlic. Heat beer in the pot until almost boiling.
2. Dredge cheese in flour and add about ½ cup at a time, stirring until cheese is melted and blended before adding more.
3. When mixture is smooth and thickened, stir in Worcestershire sauce and dry mustard.
4. Sprinkle chives on top and serve with bread cubes. Keep fondue warm while serving.

4 to 6 servings

Cheesy Potato Fondue

3 cups sliced pared potatoes
3 cups water
1 tablespoon butter
1 tablespoon flour
1½ cups milk
¾ cup coarsely grated Parmesan or Romano cheese
2 egg yolks, fork beaten
¾ teaspoon salt
⅛ teaspoon cayenne pepper
Cooked ham, cut into cubes
Cherry tomatoes, halved
Zucchini slices

1. Cook potatoes in a small amount of water until soft (about 15 minutes). Drain, reserving the water; sieve or rice potatoes.
2. Melt butter in a large fondue saucepan. Add flour and cook 1 or 2 minutes without browning.
3. Stir in potatoes with reserved water and milk. Blend until smooth and simmer 10 minutes, stirring occasionally.
4. Stir in cheese and beat in egg yolks. Continue beating until mixture is smooth, hot, and thick. Stir in salt and cayenne.
5. Serve warm with ham, tomatoes, and zucchini for dippers.

4 to 6 servings

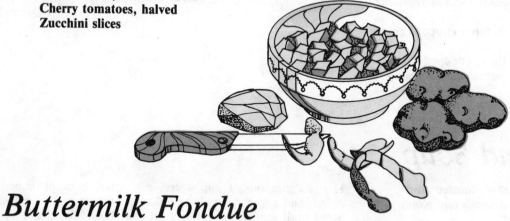

Buttermilk Fondue

1 pound Swiss cheese, shredded (about 4 cups)
3 tablespoons cornstarch
½ teaspoon salt
⅛ teaspoon white pepper
¼ teaspoon dry mustard
2 cups buttermilk
1 clove garlic, split in half
1 loaf dark rye bread, cut into 1-inch cubes

1. Toss cheese with a mixture of cornstarch, salt, pepper, and dry mustard. Set aside.
2. In a fondue saucepan, heat buttermilk with garlic over low heat. When hot, remove garlic and add cheese; stir constantly until cheese is melted.
3. Keep fondue warm over low heat while dipping bread cubes.

4 to 6 servings

Swiss Cheese Fondue

1 tablespoon cornstarch
2 tablespoons kirsch
1 clove garlic, halved
2 cups Neuchâtel or other dry
    white wine
1 pound natural Swiss cheese,
    shredded (about 4 cups)
Freshly ground black pepper to
    taste
Ground nutmeg to taste
1 loaf French bread, cut into
    1-inch cubes

1. Mix cornstarch and kirsch in a small bowl; set aside.
2. Rub the inside of a nonmetal fondue pot with cut surface of garlic. Pour in wine; place over medium heat until wine is about to simmer (do not boil).
3. Add cheese in small amounts to the hot wine, stirring constantly until cheese is melted. Heat cheese-wine mixture until bubbly.
4. Blend in cornstarch mixture and continue stirring while cooking 5 minutes, or until fondue begins to bubble; add seasoning.
5. Dip bread cubes in fondue. Keep the fondue gently bubbling throughout serving time.

About 6 servings

Creamy Corn Dip

2 tablespoons butter or margarine
2 tablespoons finely chopped green
    pepper
¼ cup flour
¼ teaspoon salt
⅛ teaspoon cayenne pepper
1½ cups chicken broth (dissolve 1
    chicken bouillon cube in 1½
    cups boiling water)
4 ounces Swiss cheese, shredded
    (about 1 cup)
1 can (8 ounces) cream-style corn
4 drops Tabasco
Party rye bread, buttered and
    toasted, or crusty French
    bread cubes

1. Heat butter in cooking pan of a chafing dish over medium heat. Add green pepper and cook until just tender, occasionally moving and turning with a spoon. Blend in flour, salt, and cayenne. Heat until mixture bubbles, stirring constantly.
2. Blend in chicken broth, cooking and stirring until sauce thickens.
3. Remove from heat. Add cheese all at one time, stirring until cheese is melted. Stir in corn and Tabasco.
4. Keep warm over hot water while serving.

About 6 servings

Rinktum Ditty with Beans

1 can (10¾ ounces) condensed
    tomato soup
8 ounces sharp Cheddar cheese,
    shredded (about 2 cups)
¼ teaspoon dry mustard
½ teaspoon Worcestershire sauce
2 drops Tabasco
1 egg, slightly beaten
2 cups cooked and drained large
    white dried beans
Salt and pepper

1. Heat soup, cheese, and seasonings over hot water in cooking pan of chafing dish.
2. When cheese is melted, quickly add beaten egg, stirring constantly until smooth. Stir in the cooked, drained beans. Season to taste.
3. Heat over simmering water until piping hot and serve over **crisp hot toast.**

About 8 servings

Note: If desired, cooked red or pinto beans may be substituted for white beans.

Tasty Rabbit

3 tablespoons butter or margarine
¼ cup flour
½ teaspoon dry mustard
1 teaspoon salt
¼ teaspoon pepper
2 cups milk
6 ounces Cheddar cheese, shredded
   (about 1½ cups)
¼ cup diced pimento
1 cup (3½ ounces) shredded dried
   beef
6 to 8 slices toast, buttered

1. Heat butter in cooking pan of a chafing dish. Remove from heat and blend in flour, dry mustard, salt, and pepper; heat and stir until bubbly.
2. Gradually add milk, stirring until smooth. Cook over medium heat, stirring constantly, until mixture thickens. Cook 1 to 2 minutes longer.
3. Place over simmering water and add cheese, stirring until melted. Stir in pimento and dried beef. Serve immediately over buttered toast.

6 to 8 servings

Welsh Rabbit with East Indian Flavor

1 tablespoon butter
1 pound sharp Cheddar cheese,
   shredded (about 4 cups)
½ teaspoon Worcestershire sauce
½ teaspoon dry mustard
   Few grains cayenne pepper
⅔ cup milk
2 tablespoons chutney
6 slices bread, toasted

1. Heat butter in cooking pan of a chafing dish over low heat. Add cheese all at one time and stir occasionally until cheese begins to melt.
2. Place over direct heat of chafing dish and blend in Worcestershire sauce, dry mustard, and cayenne pepper. Add milk gradually, stirring constantly until mixture is smooth and cheese is melted.
3. Spread a teaspoon of chutney over each slice of toast. Top with cheese mixture. Serve immediately. Top each serving with a poached egg, if desired.

6 servings

Shrimp-Walnut Rabbit

2 tablespoons butter or margarine
1 green onion including top, thinly
   sliced
1 cup thinly sliced celery
2 tablespoons flour
½ teaspoon salt
1 cup milk
   Pinch cayenne pepper
2 tablespoons dry white wine
½ cup shredded sharp Cheddar
   cheese
1 cup cleaned cooked shrimp
½ cup coarsely chopped walnuts

1. In cooking pan of a chafing dish, melt butter. Stir in onion and celery. Cook 5 minutes over medium heat.
2. Blend in flour and salt. Add milk gradually. Cook over medium heat, stirring constantly, until mixture boils and is thickened.
3. Stir in cayenne, wine, and cheese. Add shrimp and walnuts. Heat thoroughly over simmering water; do not boil.
4. Serve in heated patty shells.

4 servings

Cheese-Tomato Supper Dish

⅔ cup butter or margarine
¼ cup minced onion
1 cup mushrooms, cleaned and sliced
2 tablespoons flour
½ teaspoon dry mustard
¼ teaspoon salt
Few grains cayenne pepper
½ cup milk
½ teaspoon Worcestershire sauce
1 can (10¾ ounces) condensed tomato soup
¾ pound sharp Cheddar cheese, shredded (about 3 cups)
6 hard-cooked eggs, cut into quarters lengthwise
1 tablespoon minced parsley

1. Heat butter in cooking pan of chafing dish over medium heat. Add onion and mushrooms. Cook over medium heat, stirring occasionally, until mushrooms are tender. With a slotted spoon, remove mushrooms to a bowl; set aside.
2. Blend a mixture of flour, dry mustard, salt, and cayenne pepper into cooking pan. Heat until mixture bubbles and remove from heat.
3. Gradually add milk, Worcestershire sauce, and condensed soup while stirring. Place cooking pan over simmering water. Add cheese all at once, and stir until cheese is melted.
4. Blend in the hard-cooked eggs and reserved mushrooms. Garnish with parsley and serve with **toast fingers** or **bread sticks**.

About 8 servings

Bacon 'n' Egg Croquettes

3 tablespoons butter or margarine
2 tablespoons chopped onion
3 tablespoons flour
½ teaspoon salt
⅛ teaspoon pepper
¾ teaspoon dry mustard
¾ cup milk
6 hard-cooked eggs, coarsely chopped
8 slices bacon, cooked and finely crumbled
1 egg, fork beaten
2 tablespoons water
⅓ cup fine dry bread or cracker crumbs
Oil for deep frying

1. Melt butter in a saucepan; stir in onion and cook about 2 minutes, or until tender. Stir in a mixture of flour, salt, pepper, and dry mustard. Heat until bubbly. Add milk gradually, stirring constantly. Cook and stir until mixture forms a ball.
2. Remove from heat and stir in chopped eggs and crumbled bacon. Refrigerate about 1 hour, or until chilled.
3. Shape into 8 croquettes (balls or cones). Mix egg with water. Roll croquettes in crumbs, dip into egg, and roll again in crumbs.
4. Fill a large wok no more than half full with oil. Slowly heat to 385°F. Fry croquettes without crowding in the hot oil 2 minutes, or until golden. Remove croquettes with a slotted spoon; drain over fat and place on paper towel to drain.

4 servings

Herbed Egg Croquettes: Follow recipe for Bacon 'n' Egg Croquettes. Decrease mustard to ¼ teaspoon and bacon to 4 slices. Add ½ **teaspoon summer savory**, crushed, with mustard and **4 teaspoons snipped parsley** with chopped egg.

Cottage Cheese Croquettes

3 tablespoons butter or margarine
¼ cup flour
1 teaspoon salt
Dash pepper
½ teaspoon dill weed
1 cup milk
1 teaspoon instant minced onion
1 cup elbow macaroni, cooked and
    drained
1 pound (2 cups) creamed cottage
    cheese
1½ cups corn-flake crumbs (more
    if needed)
3 eggs, slightly beaten
    Oil for deep frying

1. In a 3-quart saucepan, melt butter. Blend in flour, salt, pepper, and dill weed.
2. Combine milk with onion. Add gradually to flour mixture, stirring constantly. Stir while cooking until thickened. Reduce heat and cook 2 minutes longer.
3. Stir in macaroni and cheese; mix well. Chill 1 to 2 hours, or until firm enough to handle.
4. Shape into 12 croquettes, coating with crumbs as soon as shaped. Dip in egg and again in crumbs.
5. Fill wok not more than half full with oil. Slowly heat oil to 375°F. Fry 3 croquettes at a time in hot oil until golden brown. Remove to a baking sheet lined with paper towels to drain. When all croquettes are drained, remove paper towels.
6. Bake croquettes at 350°F 10 to 15 minutes. Serve hot.

6 servings

Note: If desired, fine dry bread crumbs can be substituted for the corn-flake crumbs.

Eggs Creole

¼ cup chopped onion
½ cup finely diced green pepper
1 tablespoon butter or margarine
1 can (8 ounces) tomato sauce
1 jar (4 ounces) whole mushrooms,
    (undrained)
⅛ teaspoon thyme
¼ teaspoon salt
⅛ teaspoon pepper
4 eggs
    English muffins, split, toasted,
    and buttered

1. Cook onion and green pepper in butter in cooking pan of a chafing dish over medium heat about 3 minutes.
2. Add tomato sauce, mushrooms, thyme, salt, and pepper to onion and green pepper; mix well. Heat to simmering.
3. Break eggs, one at a time, into a saucer and gently slip egg into the hot mixture.
4. Simmer, covered, over low heat about 5 minutes, then place over simmering water and heat, covered, until egg whites are set.
5. To serve, place an egg on each English muffin half and top with sauce.

4 servings

Eggs Pisto Style

1 large clove garlic
1 cup thinly sliced onion
1 cup slivered green pepper
½ cup olive oil
1 cup thin raw potato strips
1 tablespoon chopped parsley
⅓ cup (2 ounces) diced cooked ham
2 cups small cubes yellow summer
    squash
2 cups finely cut peeled ripe
    tomatoes
2 teaspoons salt
1 teaspoon sugar
⅛ teaspoon pepper
6 eggs, beaten

1. Add garlic, onion, and green pepper to heated olive oil in a large wok; cook until softened, then remove garlic.
2. Add remaining ingredients except eggs to wok; cook over medium heat, stirring frequently, about 10 minutes, or until squash is just tender.
3. Pour beaten eggs into vegetables, and cook over low heat. With a spatula, lift mixture from bottom and sides as it thickens, allowing uncooked portion to flow to bottom. Cook until eggs are thick and creamy.

6 servings

Scrambled Eggs Deluxe

6 eggs
6 tablespoons milk, cream, or
    undiluted evaporated milk
¾ teaspoon salt
⅛ teaspoon pepper
½ teaspoon Worcestershire sauce
¼ cup finely shredded Cheddar
    cheese
3 tablespoons butter or margarine
1 medium-size firm ripe tomato,
    peeled and cut into small cubes
1 cup ¼- to ½-inch croutons

1. Beat eggs, milk, salt, pepper, and Worcestershire sauce together until blended. Stir in cheese.
2. Melt butter in wok over very low heat. Pour egg mixture into wok and cook over low heat. With a spatula, lift mixture from bottom and sides of wok as eggs cook, allowing uncooked portion to flow to bottom. Cook eggs until they are thick and creamy.
3. Before removing from heat, gently stir in tomato and croutons.

4 to 6 servings

Cheddar-Beer Omelet

⅓ cup beer
¼ teaspoon salt
½ teaspoon Tabasco
6 eggs
½ cup shredded Cheddar cheese
2 to 3 tablespoons butter

1. Combine beer, salt, and Tabasco in a bowl. Add eggs to mixture and beat with a rotary beater only until well blended, do not beat until frothy.
2. Place 1 tablespoon butter, more if needed, in a wok and heat. Pour in half the egg mixture and stir rapidly with a fork until mixture begins to set.
3. Sprinkle with half the cheese. When omelet is cooked but top is still moist, fold over both sides of omelet towards center and place on a warm platter while making other omelet.

4 to 6 servings

Egg Foo Yong

1 cup finely diced cooked ham,
    roast pork, or chicken
1 cup drained canned bean
    sprouts
¾ cup chopped onion
1 tablespoon soy sauce
½ teaspoon monosodium glutamate
¼ to ½ teaspoon salt (reduce if
    using ham)
6 eggs, slightly beaten
    Fat or cooking oil (about 2
    tablespoons or enough to
    form an ⅛-inch layer)
    Foo Yong Sauce

1. Mix ham, bean sprouts, onion, soy sauce, monosodium glutamate, and salt. Stir in eggs.
2. Heat fat in a large wok. Drop a fourth of the mixture into the hot fat to form a patty. Cook about 5 minutes, or until browned on one side; turn and brown other side.
3. Remove patty from wok; drain over fat a few seconds. Transfer to a warm heat-resistant platter; keep warm in a 200°F oven while cooking remaining patties.
4. Pour hot sauce over the patties and serve with **hot fluffy rice** and additional soy sauce.

4 servings

Foo Yong Sauce: Blend **2 teaspoons cornstarch, 1 tablespoon cold water, 2 teaspoons soy sauce,** and **1 teaspoon molasses** in a small saucepan. Stir in **1 cup chicken broth.** Bring to boiling, stirring constantly. Boil 3 minutes, or until sauce is thickened. Keep hot.

¾ cup sauce

MEAT

Beef à la Fondue

2 teaspoons butter
1 tablespoon flour
½ cup dry white wine
8 ounces Swiss cheese, shredded
   (about 2 cups)
1½ pounds beef top sirloin steak,
   cut into bite-size pieces
   Oil for deep frying
   Sauces for dipping

1. Melt butter in top of a double boiler over boiling water. Remove from heat; add flour and part of wine, mixing to a smooth paste.
2. Add remaining wine; heat over water until thickened. Add cheese; heat until melted. Keep warm.
3. At serving time, fill a metal fondue pot half full with oil. Heat oil to 375°F. Cook a cube of beef in the hot oil and dip it into the cheese sauce, and then into other sauces and side dishes. **Horseradish sauce** (sour cream and horseradish), **tartar sauce, mustard sauce, chopped chives** and **chutney** are suitable sauces and accompaniments. These should be in small individual dishes clustered around each place setting.

4 servings

Fondue Bourguignonne

   Sauces for dipping (three or
    or more)
   Cooking oil
1½ to 2 pounds beef tenderloin
   or sirloin, cut into 1-inch pieces

1. Prepare sauces and set aside until serving time.
2. Fill a metal fondue pot half full with oil. Heat oil to 375°F. Spear pieces of meat with dipping forks and plunge into hot oil, cooking until done as desired.
3. Dip cooked meat in desired sauce and transfer to plate. Place another piece of meat in hot oil to cook while eating cooked meat.

4 servings

Velvet Lemon Sauce

2 eggs
½ teaspoon salt
2 tablespoons lemon juice
½ cup butter, softened
   Few grains white pepper
½ slice onion
½ cup hot water

1. Put eggs, salt, lemon juice, butter, pepper, and onion into an electric blender container. Blend until smooth. Add hot water, a little at a time, while blending.
2. Turn into top of double boiler. Cook over simmering water, stirring constantly until thickened (about 10 minutes).

About 1½ cups sauce

Rémoulade Sauce

1 cup mayonnaise
1½ teaspoons prepared mustard
¼ teaspoon anchovy paste
2 tablespoons finely chopped dill
   pickles
1 tablespoon chopped capers
1½ teaspoons minced parsley
½ teaspoon finely crushed chervil
½ teaspoon crushed tarragon

Blend all ingredients in a small bowl. Cover; chill thoroughly.

About 1 cup sauce

Paprika Sauce

2 tablespoons butter or margarine
2 tablespoons flour
½ teaspoon salt
⅛ teaspoon pepper
1 cup milk
1 teaspoon minced onion
Few grains nutmeg
2 to 3 teaspoons paprika

1. Heat butter in a saucepan. Blend in flour, salt, and pepper; heat and stir until bubbly.
2. Gradually add milk, stirring until smooth. Bring to boiling; cook and stir 1 to 2 minutes longer.
3. Blend in onion, nutmeg, and paprika.

About 1 cup sauce

Jiffy Sauces for Fondue Bourguignonne

Onion-Chili: **Combine ½ envelope (about 1½ ounces) dry onion soup mix and ¾ cup boiling water** in a saucepan. Cover partially and cook 10 minutes. Adding gradually, mix in **1½ tablespoons flour** mixed with **¼ cup water.** Bring to boiling, stirring constantly; cook until thickened. Remove from heat; mix in **2 tablespoons chili sauce.**

Onion-Horseradish: Blend **½ envelope (about 1½ ounces) dry onion soup mix, 1 tablespoon milk, 2 teaspoons prepared horseradish,** and desired amount of **snipped parsley** into **1 cup dairy sour cream.**

Horseradish: Blend **3 tablespoons prepared horseradish, 1 teaspoon grated onion,** and **½ teaspoon lemon juice** with **1 cup mayonnaise.**

Curry: Blend **1 tablespoon curry powder, 1 teaspoon grated onion,** and **½ teaspoon lemon juice** with **1 cup mayonnaise.**

Mustard: Blend **1 tablespoon half-and-half** with **1 cup mayonnaise** and stir in **prepared mustard** to taste.

Caper: Mix **1 tablespoon chopped capers** and **1 cup bottled tartar sauce;** blend in **1 tablespoon half-and-half.**

Béarnaise: Blend **1 tablespoon parsley flakes, ½ teaspoon grated onion, ¼ teaspoon crushed tarragon,** and **1 teaspoon tarragon vinegar** into **hollandaise sauce** prepared from a mix according to package directions.

Barbecue: Blend **prepared horseradish** to taste with a **bottled barbecue sauce.**

Chinese Beef and Pea Pods

1½ pounds flank steak, thinly
    sliced diagonally across grain
1 to 2 tablespoons cooking oil
1 bunch green onions, chopped
    (tops included)
1 or 2 packages (7 ounces each)
    frozen Chinese pea pods,
    partially thawed to separate
1 can (10½ ounces) condensed
    beef consommé
3 tablespoons soy sauce
¼ teaspoon ground ginger
2 tablespoons cornstarch
2 tablespoons cold water
1 can (16 ounces) bean sprouts,
    drained and rinsed

1. Stir-fry meat, a third at a time, in hot oil in a large wok until browned. Remove from wok and keep warm.
2. Put green onions and pea pods into wok. Stir in a mixture of condensed consommé, soy sauce, and ginger. Bring to boiling and cook, covered, about 2 minutes.
3. Blend cornstarch with water and stir into boiling liquid in wok. Stirring constantly, boil 2 to 3 minutes. Mix in the meat and bean sprouts; heat thoroughly.
4. Serve over **hot fluffy rice.**

6 servings

Green Pepper Steak

2 pounds beef flank steak
2 tablespoons olive oil
1 teaspoon garlic salt
⅛ teaspoon black pepper
¼ teaspoon ground ginger
¼ cup soy sauce
½ teaspoon sugar
2 tomatoes, peeled and quartered
2 green peppers, cut into 1-inch
    pieces
1 can (16 ounces) bean sprouts,
    drained and rinsed
1 tablespoon cornstarch
6 tablespoons cold water

1. Cut flank steak into thin strips across the grain; set aside.
2. Heat olive oil in a large wok. Add 1 pound of meat and a mixture of garlic salt, pepper, and ginger; stir-fry over high heat until browned. Remove cooked meat and stir-fry remaining pound of meat until browned. Place all meat in wok.
3. Blend in soy sauce and sugar; cover tightly and cook slowly 5 minutes. Add tomato, green pepper, and bean sprouts; bring to boiling, cover, and cook rapidly 5 minutes.
4. Stirring constantly, blend in a mixture of cornstarch and water. Bring to boiling and cook 2 to 3 minutes, or until sauce thickens.
5. Serve with **hot fluffy rice.**

About 6 servings

Spicy Beef Strips

1½ pounds beef round steak (¼
    inch thick)
2 tablespoons cooking oil
1 clove garlic
2 beef bouillon cubes
1 cup boiling water
1 tablespoon instant minced onion
½ teaspoon salt
    Few grains cayenne pepper
¼ teaspoon chili powder
¼ teaspoon ground cinnamon
¼ teaspoon ground celery seed
2 tablespoons prepared mustard

1. Cut round steak into 2x½-inch strips; set aside.
2. Heat cooking oil in a large wok. Add garlic and stir-fry until browned. Remove the garlic.
3. Add the round steak strips, half at a time, and stir-fry until browned.
4. Dissolve bouillon cubes in boiling water. Add to wok with all the ingredients; stir to mix. Cover and simmer 25 to 30 minutes, or until meat is fork-tender.
5. Serve over **hot fluffy rice.**

6 servings

Nectarine Sukiyaki

1 tablespoon cooking oil
2 pounds beef sirloin steak,
   boneless, cut 1½ inches thick,
   sliced ¹⁄₁₆ inch thick, and cut
   into about 2½-inch pieces
2 large onions, cut in thin wedges
8 green onions (including tops),
   cut into 2-inch pieces
5 ounces fresh mushrooms, sliced
   lengthwise
1 can (5 ounces) bamboo shoots,
   drained and sliced
2 cups unpared sliced fresh
   nectarines
½ cup soy sauce
½ cup canned condensed beef broth
2 tablespoons sugar

1. Heat oil in a large wok. Add meat, 1 pound at a time, and stir-fry over high heat until browned. Remove meat and set aside.
2. Arrange vegetables and nectarines in mounds in wok; top with the beef. Pour a mixture of soy sauce, condensed beef broth, and sugar over all. Simmer 3 to 5 minutes, or until onions are just tender.
3. Serve immediately over **hot fluffy rice.**

6 to 8 servings

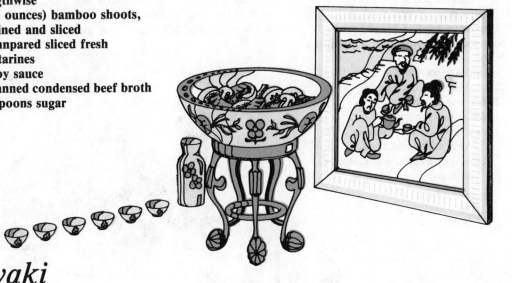

Sukiyaki

½ cup Japanese soy sauce (shoyu)
½ cup sake or sherry
⅓ cup sugar
3 tablespoons cooking oil
1½ pounds beef tenderloin, sliced ¹⁄₁₆
   inch thick and cut into pieces
   about 2½x1½ inches
12 scallions (including tops), cut
   into 2-inch lengths
½ head Chinese cabbage (cut
   lengthwise), cut into 1-inch
   pieces
½ pound spinach leaves, cut into
   1-inch strips
2 cups drained shirataki (or cold
   cooked very thin long egg
   noodles)
12 large mushrooms, sliced
   lengthwise
12 cubes tofu (soybean curd)
1 can (8½ ounces) whole bamboo
   shoots, drained and cut in large
   pieces

1. Mix soy sauce, sake, and sugar to make the sauce; set aside.
2. Heat oil in a wok and add enough sauce to form a ¼-inch layer in bottom of wok.
3. Add half the beef and stir-fry just until pink color disappears; remove and stir-fry remaining meat, adding more of the sauce if necessary. Remove meat and set aside.
4. Arrange all other ingredients in individual mounds in skillet. Top with beef.
5. Cook until vegetables are just tender. Do not stir. Serve immediately with bowls of **hot cooked rice.**

4 servings

Beef Chow Mein

2 to 4 tablespoons cooking oil
1 pound beef tenderloin or sirloin steak, cut into 3x½x⅛-inch strips
½ pound fresh mushrooms, sliced lengthwise
2 cups sliced celery
2 green onions, sliced ½ inch thick
1 small green pepper, cut into narrow strips
1½ cups boiling water
1 teaspoon salt
½ teaspoon monosodium glutamate
⅛ teaspoon pepper
2 tablespoons cold water
2 tablespoons cornstarch
2 teaspoons soy sauce
1 teaspoon sugar
1 can (16 ounces) Chinese vegetables, drained
2 tablespoons coarsely chopped pimento

1. Heat 2 tablespoons oil in a large wok. Add beef and stir-fry until browned evenly. Remove meat; set aside.
2. Heat more oil, if necessary, in wok. Stir in mushrooms, celery, green onions, and green pepper; stir-fry 1 minute. Reduce heat and blend in boiling water, salt, monosodium glutamate, and pepper. Bring to boiling; cover and simmer 2 minutes. Remove vegetables; keep warm.
3. Bring liquid in wok to boiling and stir in a blend of cold water, cornstarch, soy sauce, and sugar. Cook and stir 2 to 3 minutes. Reduce heat; mix in the browned beef, vegetables, Chinese vegetables, and pimento. Heat thoroughly.
4. Serve piping hot with **chow mein noodles.**

4 to 6 servings

Beef Stroganoff

1 pound beef tenderloin, sirloin, or rib, boneless, cut into 2x½x¼-inch strips
¼ cup flour
½ teaspoon salt
Pinch black pepper
3 tablespoons butter or margarine
¼ cup finely chopped onion
1 cup beef broth
1½ tablespoons butter or margarine
¼ pound fresh mushrooms, sliced lengthwise
½ cup dairy sour cream
1½ tablespoons tomato paste
½ teaspoon Worcestershire sauce

1. Coat meat strips evenly with a mixture of flour, salt, and pepper.
2. Heat 3 tablespoons butter in a large heavy skillet. Add meat strips and onion. Brown on all sides over medium heat, turning occasionally. Add broth; cover and simmer about 20 minutes.
3. Heat 1½ tablespoons butter in cooking pan of a chafing dish over medium heat. Add mushrooms and cook until lightly browned and tender. Add meat and liquid to mushrooms.
4. Blending well after each addition, add a mixture of sour cream, tomato paste, and Worcestershire sauce in small amounts. Place over simmering water and continue cooking, stirring constantly, until thoroughly heated (do not boil).

About 4 servings

Beef Polynesian

2 tablespoons cooking oil
1 pound lean ground beef
1 can (4 ounces) mushrooms, drained
½ cup golden raisins
1 package (10 ounces) frozen green peas
½ cup beef broth
1 teaspoon curry powder
1 tablespoon soy sauce
1 orange, sliced
½ cup salted cashews
Fried Rice

1. Heat oil in a large wok. Add ground beef and separate into small pieces; cook until lightly browned.
2. Add mushrooms, raisins, peas, broth, curry powder, and soy sauce. Break block of peas apart, if necessary, and gently toss mixture to blend.
3. Arrange orange slices over top. Cover loosely and cook over low heat 15 minutes.
4. Mix in cashews and serve with Fried Rice.

About 4 servings

Fried Rice: Cook ½ **cup chopped onion** in **2 tablespoons butter** until golden. Mix in **2 cups cooked rice** and **2 tablespoons soy sauce.** Cook over low heat, stirring occasionally, 5 minutes. Stir in **1 slightly beaten egg** and cook until set.

Deep-Fried Beef Pies

Pastry:
1 cup all-purpose flour
½ teaspoon salt
⅓ cup shortening
2 or 3 tablespoons cold water

Filling:
¾ pound lean ground beef
2 tablespoons shortening
1½ teaspoons olive oil
1 teaspoon salt
¼ teaspoon black pepper
⅛ teaspoon cayenne pepper
1 ripe tomato, peeled and cut in pieces
⅓ cup finely chopped green pepper
¼ cup finely chopped carrot
¼ cup finely chopped celery
¼ cup finely chopped onion
¼ cup finely chopped green onion
1 tablespoon chopped hot red pepper
1 tablespoon snipped parsley
1 tablespoon snipped seedless raisins
1 tablespoon chopped pitted green olives
1 tablespoon capers
¼ cup water
Oil for deep frying

1. To make pastry, sift flour and salt together into a bowl. Cut in shortening with pastry blender or two knives until pieces are the size of small peas.
2. Sprinkle water over mixture, a teaspoonful at a time, mixing lightly with a fork after each addition. Add only enough water to hold pastry together. Shape into a ball and wrap in waxed paper; chill.
3. To make filling, cook ground beef in hot shortening and olive oil in a large skillet, separating meat with a spoon. Remove from heat and drain off fat. Mix in remaining ingredients except the oil for deep frying. Cover and simmer 30 minutes.
4. Working with half the chilled pastry at a time, roll out ⅛ inch thick on a lightly floured surface. Using a lightly floured 4-inch cutter, cut into rounds. Place 1 tablespoon filling on each round. Moisten edges with cold water, fold pastry over, press edges together, and tightly seal.
5. Slowly heat the oil for deep frying in a wok to 375°F.
6. Fry one layer at a time in the heated oil until lightly browned on both sides (about 3 minutes.) Drain on absorbent paper.

About 16 pies

Stir-Fry Beef and Broccoli

2 pounds broccoli
2 pounds beef round or chuck, boneless
¼ cup olive oil
2 cloves garlic, minced
3 cups hot chicken broth
4 teaspoons cornstarch
¼ cup cold water
3 tablespoons soy sauce
1 teaspoon salt
2 cans (16 ounces each) bean sprouts, drained and rinsed

1. Cut broccoli into pieces about 2½ inches long and ¼ inch thick; set aside. Slice beef very thin and cut diagonally into 4x½-inch strips; set aside.
2. Heat 1 tablespoon olive oil with garlic in a large wok. Add half the beef and stir-fry until evenly browned. Remove cooked meat from the wok and stir-fry remaining beef, adding more olive oil, if necessary.
3. Pour 1 tablespoon olive oil in the wok. Add half the broccoli and stir-fry over high heat ½ minute. Remove cooked broccoli from the wok and stir-fry remaining broccoli ½ minute, adding more oil, if necessary.
4. Place all the broccoli in the wok; cover and cook 3 minutes. Remove broccoli and keep warm.
5. Blend into broth a mixture of cornstarch, cold water, soy sauce, and salt. Bring to boiling, stirring constantly, and cook until mixture thickens.
6. Add bean sprouts, broccoli, and beef; toss to mix. Heat thoroughly and serve over **hot fluffy rice.**

8 servings

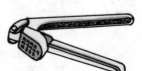

Hamburger Stroganoff

1½ pounds lean ground beef
2 large onions, sliced
2 cans (10½ ounces each) condensed cream of chicken soup
1 pint dairy sour cream
1 teaspoon salt
Dash black pepper

1. Sauté ground beef and onions in a small amount of fat in cooking pan of a chafing dish until meat is well browned.
2. Stir in condensed soup, sour cream, salt, and pepper.
3. Cook, covered, over direct heat of chafing dish until thoroughly heated.

About 6 servings

Sloppy Joe Fondue

1 tablespoon butter or margarine
1 pound ground beef
1 envelope (about 1½ ounces) Sloppy Joe seasoning mix
1 can (6 ounces) tomato paste
Water
⅓ cup chopped celery
¼ cup chopped green pepper

1. Heat butter in a large skillet. Add meat and brown, breaking into small pieces with a spoon. Stir in seasoning mix, tomato paste, and water called for in package directions. Mix in celery and green pepper. Bring to boiling, stirring occasionally.
2. Reduce heat, cover, and simmer 10 minutes, stirring occasionally.
3. Turn into a fondue saucepan and keep warm.
4. To serve, spoon over halves of **toasted buttered buns** or **English muffins.**

4 servings

Embassy Veal Glacé

1½ teaspoons dry tarragon leaves
 1 cup dry white wine
1½ pounds veal round steak (about ¼ inch thick)
 3 tablespoons butter or margarine
 ½ teaspoon salt
 ⅛ teaspoon pepper
 ½ cup condensed beef consommé
 ½ cup dry vermouth

1. Stir tarragon into white wine; cover and set aside several hours, stirring occasionally.
2. Cut meat into pieces about 3x2 inches. Heat butter in cooking pan of chafing dish until lightly browned. Add meat and lightly brown on both sides; season with salt and pepper.
3. Reduce heat and pour in tarragon-wine mixture with the consommé and vermouth. Simmer, uncovered, about 10 minutes, or until veal is tender.
4. Remove veal to a platter and cover.
5. Increase heat under pan and cook sauce until it is reduced to a thin glaze, stirring occasionally. Return veal to pan and spoon sauce over meat, turning meat once.
6. Cover and place over direct heat of chafing dish until warm.

About 6 servings

Veal Scaloppine with Mushrooms

 1 tablespoon flour
 ¾ teaspoon salt
   Pinch pepper
 1 pound veal cutlets
 2 tablespoons cooking oil
 4 ounces fresh mushrooms, quartered lengthwise
 ½ cup sherry
 2 tablespoons finely chopped parsley

1. Combine flour, salt, and pepper; sprinkle over veal slices. Pound slices until thin, flat, and round, working flour mixture into both sides. Cut into ¼-inch-wide strips.
2. Heat oil in a large wok. Add veal strips and stir-fry over high heat until golden.
3. Sprinkle mushrooms on top and pour sherry over all. Simmer, uncovered, about 15 minutes, or until tender.
4. Toss with parsley and serve.

4 servings

Orange Pork Chops

 1 cup orange juice
 3 tablespoons instant minced onion
 2 teaspoons grated orange peel
 1 tablespoon brown sugar
 ½ teaspoon marjoram, crushed
 ¼ teaspoon thyme, crushed
 4 pork chops, cut about 1 inch thick
 ½ teaspoon salt
 ⅛ teaspoon pepper
   Cooking oil
   Oranges, pared and sectioned

1. Combine orange juice, onion, orange peel, brown sugar, marjoram, and thyme; set aside.
2. Season pork chops with salt and pepper. Brown chops well on both sides in a small amount of oil in a heavy skillet.
3. Place chops in cooking pan of a chafing dish. Add orange juice mixture. Cook, covered, over low heat about 45 minutes, or until chops are very tender. If desired, thicken the sauce slightly with a cornstarch-water mixture.
4. Add orange sections and heat 5 to 10 minutes over direct heat of chafing dish.

4 servings

Fried Eggplant with Pork

1 medium eggplant
¼ to ½ teaspoon salt
⅓ to ½ cup cooking oil
⅛ to ¼ teaspoon ground ginger
1 clove garlic, crushed in a garlic press
½ pound pork tenderloin, cut into ¼-inch slices
¼ teaspoon salt
¼ teaspoon seasoned pepper
½ teaspoon monosodium glutamate
1 teaspoon cornstarch
1 teaspoon sugar
½ cup cold water
2 teaspoons soy sauce

1. Pare eggplant and cut into 2x1x1-inch pieces. Sprinkle with ¼ to ½ teaspoon salt.
2. Heat oil in a large wok. Stir in ginger. Cook eggplant in hot oil until partially tender (about 5 minutes). Remove eggplant with slotted spoon; set aside and keep warm.
3. If necessary, add more oil to wok and heat with garlic. Add pork and fry slices a few minutes on each side.
4. Stir a mixture of ¼ teaspoon salt, seasoned pepper, monosodium glutamate, cornstarch, and sugar into a blend of water and soy sauce. Add to wok, bring rapidly to boiling and cook 2 minutes, stirring the mixture constantly.
5. Return eggplant to wok. Cook mixture about 5 minutes, or until pork and eggplant are completely tender.
6. Just before serving, sprinkle with **minced parsley**. Transfer to a heated serving dish.

About 4 servings

Oriental Pork and Noodles

½ to 1 tablespoon cooking oil
½ teaspoon salt
1 teaspoon ground ginger or 2 thin slices ginger root, peeled and minced
1 pound lean boneless pork, thinly sliced
1 can (13¾ ounces) beef broth
2 tablespoons cornstarch
½ cup cold water
1 tablespoon soy sauce
1½ tablespoons dry sherry
1 can (5 ounces) water chestnuts, sliced
8 ounces medium noodles, cooked and drained

1. Heat oil in a large wok over high heat. Stir in salt and ginger. Add half of the pork and stir-fry 5 minutes, or until browned. Push up on sides and brown remaining pork.
2. Pour beef broth over pork and cook, covered, about 3 minutes.
3. Mix cornstarch, water, soy sauce, and sherry. Stir into pork and cook until sauce thickens.
4. Add water chestnuts and drained noodles; mix well and heat thoroughly.

6 servings

Quick Sweet and Sour Pork

1½ pounds pork, boneless, cut into 1-inch cubes
1 to 2 tablespoons cooking oil
Salt and pepper
1 can (20 ounces) pineapple chunks
½ cup bottled barbecue sauce
¼ cup vinegar
1 tablespoon cornstarch
1 large green pepper, cut into strips

1. Brown meat in hot oil in a large wok. Season meat with salt and pepper.
2. Drain juice from pineapple into a bowl and set fruit aside. Combine pineapple juice, barbecue sauce, vinegar, and cornstarch; blend thoroughly. Add to meat in wok and stir until blended.
3. Simmer, covered, about 35 minutes. Add pineapple and green pepper; simmer 10 minutes.
4. Serve over **hot fluffy rice**.

About 6 servings

Pork Mandarin

2 to 3   tablespoons cooking oil
1½   pounds pork, boneless, ¼ inch thick and cut into 2x¼-inch strips
2   teaspoons salt
¼   cup cornstarch
½   cup cold water
2   tablespoons soy sauce
1   can (about 15 ounces) pineapple chunks, drained (reserve syrup)
1   can (11 ounces) mandarin oranges, drained (reserve syrup)
1   can (12 ounces) apricot nectar
½   cup cider vinegar
¾   cup lightly packed brown sugar
1   cup diced celery
1   large green pepper, cut in strips
1   can (16 ounces) whole tomatoes, drained and quartered
12   blanched almonds, toasted

1. Heat oil in a large wok. Add pork and stir-fry until well browned on all sides. Season with salt; cover and cook until pork is done (10 to 15 minutes).
2. Blend cornstarch and water in a saucepan; stir in soy sauce, reserved syrup from fruits, apricot nectar, vinegar, and brown sugar. Bring mixture to boiling, stirring constantly; cook 3 minutes.
3. Add celery and pineapple chunks to meat. Add the sauce and cook over low heat about 5 minutes.
4. Stir in green pepper and tomato pieces and heat about 5 minutes longer.
5. Before serving, add mandarin oranges to mixture. Remove to heated serving dish and top with almonds. Serve with **hot fluffy rice.**

About 6 servings

Pork and Vegetables with Soy Sauce

6   loin pork chops
  Soy sauce
  Salt and pepper
2   bunches watercress, broken into small pieces
1   cup finely chopped green onions
3   medium-size firm tomatoes, chopped into very small pieces
½ to ¾   cup soy sauce

1. Trim all fat from chops and cut chops into small pieces.
2. Heat several pieces of fat in a wok; stir in meat.
3. When meat starts to brown, sprinkle with desired amounts of soy sauce, salt, and pepper and continue browning.
4. Meanwhile, in a large bowl, combine watercress, green onions, and tomatoes. When the pork is thoroughly cooked, toss it with the vegetables and soy sauce like a salad.
5. Serve over **hot fluffy rice.**

6 servings

Peach 'n' Pork Chop Barbecue

6   pork chops, cut 1 inch thick
1   tablespoon fat
¼   cup lightly packed brown sugar
1   teaspoon ground cinnamon
½   teaspoon ground cloves
1   can (8 ounces) tomato sauce
6   canned cling peach halves, drained (reserve ¼ cup syrup)
¼   cup cider vinegar
1   teaspoon salt
¼   teaspoon pepper

1. Brown chops on both sides in hot fat in a large heavy skillet.
2. Meanwhile, blend a mixture of brown sugar, cinnamon, and cloves with tomato sauce, reserved peach syrup, and vinegar.
3. Place pork chops in cooking pan of chafing dish. Sprinkle with salt and pepper. Place a peach half on each chop. Pour sauce over all.
4. Cover skillet and simmer about 30 minutes, or until pork is tender; baste occasionally with the sauce.

6 servings

Nutted Sweet and Sour Pork

1 tablespoon peanut oil
1 pound pork loin, boneless, cut into 3x¼x⅛-inch strips
2 medium-size green peppers, cut into 1-inch squares
⅓ cup diagonally sliced green onion
1 can (8¾ ounces) apricot halves, drained (reserve syrup)
3 tablespoons vinegar
2 tablespoons soy sauce
1 small clove garlic, minced
⅛ teaspoon ground ginger
¼ cup peanuts
1 tablespoon cornstarch
2 tablespoons water
2 cups hot cooked rice
¼ cup chopped peanuts

1. In a large wok, heat the peanut oil. Add half the meat and stir-fry until browned. Push the browned meat up on sides of wok and stir-fry remaining meat until browned. Push meat up on sides of wok.
2. Add green pepper and onion to wok. Cook over medium heat about 5 minutes, stirring occasionally. Stir meat into cooked vegetables.
3. Combine reserved apricot syrup, vinegar, soy sauce, garlic, ginger, and ¼ cup peanuts. Stir into meat mixture.
4. Simmer, covered, about 30 minutes, or until pork is tender; stir occasionally.
5. Blend cornstarch with water and stir into sauce in wok. Cook and stir until thickened. Stir in apricots and heat thoroughly.
6. Combine rice and chopped peanuts. Serve pork over rice.

4 servings

Dutch Sausage with Gravy

1 pound bulk pork sausage
1 to 2 tablespoons water
1 small onion, minced
1 tablespoon flour
1 cup beef broth

1. Shape sausage into 4 to 6 flat cakes. Put sausage cakes into a skillet. Add water; cover tightly and cook slowly about 5 minutes. Remove cover and cook slowly until well browned on both sides.
2. Remove cakes to cooking pan of a chafing dish and keep warm.
3. Drain off all but 3 tablespoons fat from skillet. Brown onion in the fat. Stir in flour and cook 1 minute. Stir in broth; simmer 5 minutes.
4. Pour gravy over sausage cakes and heat thoroughly.

4 to 6 servings

Sausage, Hominy, and Tomato Scramble

1 pound bulk pork sausage
½ cup fine dry bread crumbs
⅔ cup undiluted evaporated milk
½ teaspoon rubbed sage
¼ cup flour
2 cans (16 ounces each) tomatoes
1 can (20 ounces) hominy, drained
1 teaspoon salt
¼ teaspoon rubbed sage

1. Combine sausage, bread crumbs, evaporated milk, and ½ teaspoon sage. Mix well and shape into 16 balls. Roll balls in flour to coat, reserving remaining flour.
2. In cooking pan of a chafing dish, brown meatballs over low heat, turning frequently.
3. Remove all but 3 tablespoons of the fat from the pan. Stir in reserved flour, tomatoes, hominy, salt, and sage; blend well.
4. Cook, covered, over low heat about 15 minutes, or until sauce is thickened. Keep warm over chafing dish burner until ready to serve.

6 to 8 servings

Chinatown Chop Suey

1¼ pounds pork, boneless
1 pound beef, boneless
¾ pound veal, boneless
3 tablespoons cooking oil
1 cup water
3 cups diagonally sliced celery
2 cups coarsely chopped onion
3 tablespoons cornstarch
¼ cup water
¼ cup soy sauce
¼ cup bead molasses
1 can (16 ounces) bean sprouts,
    drained and rinsed
2 cans (5 ounces each) water
    chestnuts, drained and sliced

1. Cut meat into 2x½x¼-inch strips. Heat oil in a large wok. Stir-fry ½ pound of meat at a time, browning pieces on all sides. Remove the meat from the wok as it is browned. When all the meat is browned, return it to the wok. Cover and cook over low heat 30 minutes.
2. Mix in 1 cup water, celery, and onions. Bring to boiling and simmer, covered, 20 minutes.
3. Blend cornstarch, the ¼ cup water, soy sauce, and molasses. Stir into meat mixture. Bring to boiling and cook 2 minutes, stirring constantly. Mix in bean sprouts and water chestnuts; heat.
4. Serve on **hot fluffy rice.**

8 servings

Wok Gumbo

2 cups cooked ham, diced
1 cup chopped green pepper
1 medium onion, sliced
½ pound okra, cut in 1-inch pieces
1 can (16 ounces) tomatoes
    (undrained)
1 cup water
½ teaspoon salt
⅛ teaspoon pepper
1 cup uncooked rice

1. Combine all ingredients except rice in a large wok. Bring to boiling, cover, and simmer 10 minutes.
2. Stir in rice, cover, and simmer 20 minutes, or until rice is tender.

4 to 6 servings

Lemon Chop Suey

1 tablespoon cooking oil
1 pound chop suey meat (pork,
    beef, and veal)
½ cup chopped onion
3 cups water
½ cup sugar
2 tablespoons cornstarch
1 teaspoon salt
1 teaspoon grated lemon peel
2 tablespoons lemon juice
2 tablespoons soy sauce
1 can (16 ounces) bean sprouts,
    drained and rinsed
1 cup diagonally sliced celery
8 ounces medium noodles

1. Heat oil in a large wok. Stir-fry pork and push up on sides as it browns. Stir-fry beef, then veal, in same way.
2. Add onion and stir-fry to brown lightly. Add water and simmer, uncovered, until meat is tender (about 1 hour).
3. In last few minutes of cooking, blend sugar, cornstarch, salt, lemon peel and juice, and soy sauce until smooth. Add to meat and stir over low heat until thickened (1 or 2 minutes).
4. Stir in bean sprouts and celery. Heat thoroughly.
5. Meanwhile, cook noodles in boiling salted water until tender, yet firm (about 4 minutes). Drain and serve hot with the chop suey.

4 to 6 servings

POULTRY

Batter-Fried Chicken

1 broiler-fryer, cut into serving
   pieces
1½ cups sifted flour
½ teaspoon salt
   Dash pepper
1½ teaspoons baking powder
1 egg, beaten
1½ cups milk
   Oil for deep frying

1. Steam chicken (see instructions, page 7) in a large wok until tender. Dry and refrigerate until time to fry.
2. Just before frying the chicken, combine the dry ingredients. Blend the egg with milk and combine the liquid with the dry ingredients.
3. Slowly heat oil in a wok to 375°F. Sprinkle chicken pieces with salt and pepper. Dip chicken in batter, allow excess to drain off, and fry a few pieces at a time until brown. Drain and serve either hot or cold.

2 to 4 servings

Chicken Fondue

   Cooking oil
1 teaspoon salt
2 pounds chicken breasts, skinned,
   boned, and cut into ¾-inch
   cubes
   Sauces for dipping

1. Pour cooking oil into a metal fondue pot, not more than half full. Heat on range to 425°F. Add salt.
2. Transfer to fondue heating element. Spear chicken cube with a fondue fork and cook in hot oil 2 to 3 minutes.
3. Dip in desired sauce.

4 servings

Note: To maintain a high enough cooking temperature, it may be necessary to return pot to kitchen range and heat oil.

Easy Tomato Sauce

1 medium clove garlic, crushed in
   a garlic press
1 teaspoon oregano
½ teaspoon thyme
1 can (8 ounces) tomato sauce
3 tablespoons grated Parmesan
   cheese
   Salt and pepper to taste

Combine all ingredients in a saucepan and simmer, uncovered, 5 minutes.

Béarnaise Sauce

4 egg yolks
1 cup butter
1 tablespoon lemon juice
1 tablespoon tarragon vinegar
¼ teaspoon salt
1 teaspoon chopped parsley
1 teaspoon onion juice
   Dash cayenne pepper

1. Blend egg yolks with a third of the butter in a fondue saucepan. Place over low heat. Add remaining butter as sauce thickens, stirring constantly.
2. Remove from heat and add remaining ingredients.

1 cup sauce

Jiffy Curry Sauce

⅔ cup condensed cream of celery
   soup
1½ teaspoons instant minced onion
½ teaspoon curry powder
6 tablespoons milk
1 egg, slightly beaten
1½ teaspoons butter or margarine

1. Combine soup, onion, and curry powder in a fondue saucepan; stir until well blended. Stir in milk. Heat thoroughly over low heat, stirring occasionally.
2. Stir about ¼ cup of the hot sauce into the beaten egg; immediately return mixture to fondue saucepan.
3. Cook over low heat 3 to 5 minutes, stirring occasionally to keep mixture cooking evenly. Blend in the butter.

About 1 cup sauce

Good Fortune Chicken with Pineapple Piquant

1 egg, fork beaten
⅓ cup water
1 tablespoon milk
¼ cup flour
1 tablespoon cornstarch
1 tablespoon cornmeal
⅛ teaspoon baking powder
12 small chicken legs
   Oil for deep frying heated to
   365°F
1 tablespoon cooking oil
½ cup green pepper chunks
½ cup onion chunks
1 can (about 15 ounces) pineapple
   chunks (reserve syrup)
½ cup cider vinegar
½ cup packed brown sugar
2 tablespoons soy sauce
¼ cup water
1 tablespoon cornstarch

1. Beat egg, water, and milk with a mixture of flour, cornstarch, cornmeal, and baking powder in a bowl until smooth. Dip each chicken leg into the batter and drain over bowl a few seconds.
2. Fry pieces in hot oil 15 minutes, or until chicken is crisp-brown and tender. Remove with a slotted spoon and drain over fat; place on absorbent paper.
3. Meanwhile, heat 1 tablespoon cooking oil in a large wok, and cook green pepper and onion until crisp-tender, stirring occasionally. Push vegetables up on sides of wok.
4. Pour in reserved pineapple syrup; add vinegar, brown sugar, soy sauce, and a mixture of water and cornstarch. Stir until blended. Mix in pineapple. Bring rapidly to boiling, stirring constantly; cook 3 minutes.
5. Pour sauce over chicken legs and serve. If desired, add 1 tablespoon sesame seed to sauce, or sprinkle over chicken when served.

4 to 6 servings

Cherried Chicken

2 large chicken breasts, skinned
   and boned
3 to 4 tablespoons flour
½ teaspoon salt
¼ teaspoon paprika
⅛ teaspoon curry powder
2 to 3 tablespoons butter
½ cup dry white wine
1 can (8¼ ounces) pitted dark
   sweet cherries, drained
¼ cup pineapple chunks

1. Dredge chicken in a mixture of flour, salt, paprika, and curry powder. Heat butter in cooking pan of a chafing dish. Cook chicken slowly in the butter until golden brown on all sides.
2. Add wine and cover pan tightly. Simmer 30 minutes, or until chicken is tender.
3. Add cherries and pineapple. Heat over simmering water until heated through.

2 servings

Oriental Chicken Fondue

3 cups chicken broth or bouillon
2 pounds chicken breasts, skinned, boned, and cut into paper-thin strips
Sauces for dipping

1. Heat chicken broth to boiling. Adjust heat so broth will continue to boil gently throughout dipping.
2. Spear chicken strip with a fondue fork and cook in boiling broth 2 to 3 minutes, or until chicken turns white and is tender.
3. Transfer cooked piece of chicken to plate and start cooking another before dipping in desired sauce.

4 servings

Teriyaki Sauce

½ cup pineapple juice
¼ cup brown sugar
2 tablespoons soy sauce
1 tablespoon cooking oil
¾ teaspoon ground ginger
¼ teaspoon salt
1 clove garlic, minced

Combine all ingredients in a saucepan. Heat to blend flavors.

About ⅔ cup sauce

Tangy Plum Sauce

1 can or jar (17 ounces) purple plums, drained (reserve syrup)
½ cup frozen orange juice concentrate, thawed
½ teaspoon Worcestershire sauce

Pit plums, and force through a sieve or food mill into a bowl. Blend in reserved syrup, orange juice, and Worcestershire sauce. Heat just to blend flavors.

About 1½ cups sauce

Mustard Sauce

1 cup undiluted evaporated milk
2 tablespoons dry mustard
¼ cup sugar
3 egg yolks, well beaten
⅓ cup cider vinegar

1. Scald evaporated milk in top of a double boiler over boiling water. Blend a small amount of hot evaporated milk with dry mustard until smooth; return to remaining evaporated milk along with sugar and stir until sugar is dissolved. Add a small amount of the hot mixture to the beaten egg yolks, blending well, and return to double-boiler top.
2. Cook over boiling water about 3 minutes, stirring constantly.
3. Remove from heat. Mix in vinegar. Serve hot.

About 1¼ cups sauce

Chicken with Almonds

2 tablespoons cooking oil
⅓ cup chopped onion
1 cup chopped celery
1 can (4 ounces) mushrooms, liquid included
2 cups diced cooked chicken
1 can (5 ounces) water chestnuts, drained and sliced
2 tablespoons cornstarch
¼ teaspoon ground ginger
3 tablespoons soy sauce
¾ cup chicken bouillon
½ cup toasted almonds

1. Heat oil in a large wok. Add onion and celery; cook until soft. Stir in mushrooms and chicken and heat gently, stirring occasionally. Mix in water chestnuts and push mixture up on sides of wok.
2. Combine cornstarch, ginger, soy sauce, and bouillon. Stir into liquid in middle of wok. Cook until sauce thickens, stirring constantly.
3. When sauce thickens, combine with chicken mixture and almonds. Serve immediately over **hot fluffy rice.**

6 servings

Note: If desired, cashew nuts may be used instead of almonds.

Chicken Tokay

6 chicken breasts (about 4 pounds),
    skinned, boned, and split
1½ teaspoons salt
¼ teaspoon pepper
1 teaspoon crushed rosemary
3 tablespoons butter or margarine
¼ cup chopped onion
2 chicken bouillon cubes
1 cup boiling water
1 tablespoon lemon juice
4 teaspoons cornstarch
2 tablespoons cold water
1½ cups seeded and halved Tokay
    grapes (about 1 pound)

1. Rub chicken breasts with a mixture of the salt, pepper, and rosemary. Brown chicken slowly and evenly in hot butter in a large wok, pushing chicken up on sides of wok as it is browned.
2. Stir the onion into center of wok and cook until lightly browned, stirring occasionally. Stir chicken into onion.
3. Dissolve bouillon cubes in the boiling water and combine with lemon juice. Pour over chicken and onion. Cover and simmer until chicken is tender when pierced with a fork (about 20 minutes). Remove chicken from wok; keep hot.
4. Blend cornstarch with cold water. Stir into liquid in wok, blending thoroughly. Bring rapidly to boiling and boil 3 minutes, stirring constantly. Add grapes and chicken to wok and spoon sauce over all. Heat to serving temperature and serve immediately sprinkled with snipped **parsley**.

About 6 servings

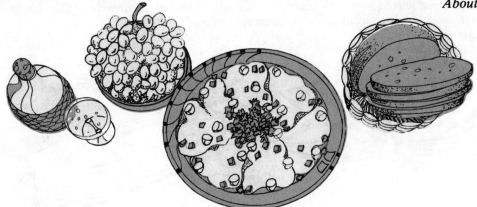

Chicken with Vegetables

4 chicken breasts, skinned and
    boned
¾ pound lean pork
3 cups chicken broth
3 tablespoons cornstarch
1 tablespoon soy sauce
1½ teaspoons salt
3 tablespoons cooking oil
2 cloves garlic, minced
3 tablespoons soy sauce
1 tablespoon sugar
¾ teaspoon sesame seed
⅛ teaspoon pepper
3 cups thinly sliced Chinese
    cabbage
3 cups thinly sliced celery
1½ cups sliced fresh mushrooms
1½ cups sliced canned bamboo
    shoots
¾ cups sliced canned water
    chestnuts

1. Cut chicken and pork into strips about 3x½x⅛ inch; set aside. Combine 3 tablespoons of the chicken broth, cornstarch, 1 tablespoon soy sauce, and salt; set aside.
2. Heat oil in a large wok until very hot. Stir in garlic. Add the chicken and pork strips; brown and cook quickly; remove from wok.
3. In the wok, mix together 3 tablespoons soy sauce, sugar, sesame seed, and pepper. Add vegetables and cook over high heat 3 minutes, tossing constantly. Add remaining chicken broth and cook 2 minutes more. Remove from heat, and using a slotted spoon, remove vegetables to a bowl and keep warm.
4. Blend the cornstarch mixture into liquid in wok, stirring constantly. Bring to boiling and boil 3 minutes, or until mixture thickens.
5. Return meat and vegetables to the wok and heat just until thoroughly heated.

6 to 8 servings

Oriental Pineapple Chicken

12 chicken wings
½ teaspoon monosodium glutamate
¼ teaspoon ground ginger
2 tablespoons cooking oil
1 clove garlic, minced
   Chicken broth (about 1½ cups)
1 can (8½ ounces) pineapple
     slices (reserve syrup)
½ cup soy sauce
2 tablespoons cider vinegar
2 tablespoons cornstarch
1 cup diagonally sliced celery
4 green onions, diagonally sliced
1 can (5 ounces) water chestnuts,
     drained and halved
1 can (16 ounces) bean sprouts,
     drained and rinsed
¼ cup toasted blanched almonds

1. Remove and discard tips from chicken wings; cut wings in half at joint. Toss with a mixture of monosodium glutamate and ginger.
2. Heat oil in a large wok and stir in garlic. Brown the chicken pieces.
3. Add enough chicken broth to the pineapple syrup to make 1⅔ cups liquid; gradually pour into the wok. Cover and simmer 15 minutes, or until wings are tender.
4. Push chicken up on sides of wok. Stir in a mixture of soy sauce, vinegar, and cornstarch. Add celery and green onion. Bring to boiling and cook 3 minutes, stirring constantly. Mix in water chestnuts, bean sprouts, almonds, and 2 pineapple slices, cut in large pieces. Move chicken through mixture. Heat thoroughly.
5. Turn into a heated serving dish. Garnish with remaining pineapple slices.

4 servings

Chicken Livers Superb

2 pounds chicken livers
¼ cup flour
1 cup finely chopped onion
½ cup butter
5 ounces fresh mushrooms,
     cleaned, sliced lengthwise
     through stems and caps, and
     lightly browned in butter
2 tablespoons Worcestershire sauce
2 tablespoons chili sauce
1 teaspoon salt
¼ teaspoon pepper
½ teaspoon rosemary
½ teaspoon thyme
2 cups dairy sour cream

1. Rinse and drain chicken livers. Pat free of excess moisture with absorbent paper. Coat lightly with flour. Set aside.
2. Lightly brown onion in heated butter in a large skillet, stirring occasionally. Remove half the onion-butter mixture and set aside for second frying of livers. Add half the chicken livers and cook, occasionally moving and turning with a spoon, about 5 minutes, or until lightly browned. Turn into the cooking pan of a chafing dish. Fry remaining livers, using all the onion-butter mixture; turn into the cooking pan. Set aside.
3. After browning mushrooms, blend a mixture of Worcestershire sauce, chili sauce, salt, pepper, rosemary, and thyme with the mushrooms. Heat thoroughly.
4. Adding sour cream in small amounts at a time and stirring constantly, quickly blend with mushroom mixture. Heat thoroughly (do not boil). Mix gently with livers to coat.
5. Set cooking pan over simmering water. Before serving, garnish with wreaths of **sieved hard-cooked egg white, watercress, and sieved hard-cooked egg yolk.** Serve with buttered toasted **English muffins.**

About 8 servings

Note: If desired, blend in ¼ cup dry sauterne or sherry with the sour cream.

Chicken Croquettes

5 to 6 tablespoons butter or
 margarine
5 to 6 tablespoons flour
 ¼ teaspoon salt
 Few grains pepper
 1½ cups milk
 2 cups finely chopped or ground
 cooked chicken
 1 tablespoon finely chopped
 parsley
 1 tablespoon lemon juice
 ½ teaspoon onion juice
 ½ teaspoon salt
 ¼ teaspoon celery salt
 1 cup fine dry bread crumbs
 1 egg, slightly beaten
 1 tablespoon milk
 Oil for deep frying

1. Heat butter in saucepan over low heat. Blend in flour, salt, and pepper. Heat until mixture is bubbly. Remove from heat and gradually stir in milk.
2. Cook rapidly, stirring constantly, until sauce thickens. Cook 1 to 2 minutes longer.
3. Mix together lightly the chicken, parsley, lemon juice, onion juice, salt, and celery salt. Combine with the sauce. Refrigerate until chilled.
4. Shape chilled mixture into balls, cones, or cylinders. Roll in bread crumbs, then dip in a mixture of the egg and milk. Roll again in bread crumbs, shaking off loose crumbs.
5. Slowly heat oil in a wok to 375°F. Deep-fry the croquettes, a few at a time, turning frequently to brown evenly. Drain on absorbent paper and serve immediately.

6 servings

Chicken in a Wok

 1 cup sliced celery, including leaves
 1 tablespoon cooking oil
 2 cups diced cooked chicken or
 turkey
 1 package (10 ounces) frozen
 carrots and peas, partially
 thawed
 ¾ cup chicken broth
 1 tablespoon cornstarch
 1 tablespoon Japanese soy sauce
 Pinch pepper

1. Cook celery in hot oil in a large wok about 3 minutes. Add chicken and brown slightly. Stir in carrots and peas and half of broth.
2. Cook, covered, over low heat about 10 minutes. Combine remaining broth with cornstarch and soy sauce. Stir into wok and add pepper. Cook until sauce thickens.

4 servings

Mexican Chicken

 2 tablespoons cooking oil
 1 cup slivered almonds
 1 cup chopped onion
 1 medium clove garlic, minced
 ⅛ teaspoon cinnamon
 ⅛ teaspoon cloves
 ¼ teaspoon pepper
 1 ounce (1 square) unsweetened
 chocolate, coarsely chopped
 2 cans (7 ounces each) green
 chili sauce
 1 can (15 ounces) tomato sauce
 2 cups bite-size pieces cooked
 chicken or turkey

1. In cooking pan of a chafing dish, heat the oil, Sauté almonds, onion, and garlic 10 minutes over medium heat, stirring often.
2. Stir in remaining ingredients except chicken. Heat, stirring, until chocolate melts. Purée mixture in a blender or force through a food mill.
3. Return mixture to cooking pan and stir in chicken. Simmer 5 minutes.
4. Serve over **hot fluffy rice**. Garnish with **avocado** or **orange slices, dairy sour cream,** or **slivered almonds.**

4 servings

Chicken Curry with Rice

⅓ cup butter or margarine
3 tablespoons chopped onion
3 tablespoons chopped celery
3 tablespoons chopped green
    apple
12 peppercorns
1 bay leaf
⅓ cup sifted flour
2½ teaspoons curry powder
½ teaspoon monosodium glutamate
¼ teaspoon sugar
Pinch nutmeg
2½ cups milk
2 teaspoons lemon juice
½ teaspoon Worcestershire sauce
3 cups cubed cooked chicken
¼ cup cream
2 tablespoons sherry
¼ teaspoon Worcestershire sauce

1. Heat butter in a heavy saucepan over low heat. Add onion, celery, apple, peppercorns, and bay leaf. Cook over medium heat until lightly browned, stirring occasionally.
2. Blend in a mixture of flour, curry powder, monosodium glutamate, sugar, and nutmeg. Heat until mixture bubbles. Remove from heat and gradually add milk, stirring constantly.
3. Return pan to heat and bring sauce rapidly to boiling. Stirring constantly, cook until sauce thickens; cook 1 to 2 minutes longer. Remove from heat and stir in lemon juice and Worcestershire sauce. Strain sauce through a fine sieve, pressing vegetables against sieve to extract all the sauce.
4. Transfer the sauce to cooking pan of a chafing dish and place over simmering water. Blend cream, sherry, and Worcestershire sauce into the warm sauce. Add cubed chicken and cook, covered, until mixture is thoroughly heated.
5. Serve with **hot fluffy rice**, and curry condiments such as **preserved kumquats, chutney, shredded coconut,** and **finely chopped roasted peanuts.**

4 servings

Chinese Chicken Crepes

16 crepes
2 tablespoons butter or margarine
½ cup thinly sliced green onion
1 cup cooked rice
¼ cup chopped parsley
1 can (8 ounces) water chestnuts,
    drained and sliced
2 cups bite-size pieces cooked
    chicken
1 teaspoon lemon juice
Chinese Sauce

1. Prepare crepes and set aside.
2. Melt butter in a large skillet. Add green onion and rice. Cook 5 minutes over low heat, stirring occasionally.
3. Stir in parsley, water chestnuts, chicken, and lemon juice. Remove from heat and stir in 1 cup Chinese Sauce.
4. Spoon a heaping ¼ cup of chicken filling onto one end of each crepe on the unbrowned side. Roll up crepes and set aside.
5. Heat about half the remaining Chinese Sauce in the cooking pan of a chafing dish. Add half the filled crepes and heat over simmering water. As crepes are heated, serve them, and place other crepes in the sauce to heat.

8 servings

Basic Crepes

1 cup all-purpose flour
⅛ teaspoon salt
3 eggs
1½ cups milk
2 tablespoons melted butter or oil

1. Sift flour and salt. Add eggs, one at a time, beating thoroughly. Gradually add milk, mixing until blended. Add melted butter or oil and beat until smooth. (Or mix in an electric blender until smooth.)
2. Let batter stand for 1 hour before cooking crepes.
3. Heat a 7-inch skillet or crepe pan over moderately high heat. Grease lightly. Pour 3 tablespoons batter into pan and tilt pan with a swirling motion to cover bottom evenly. When brown on first side, turn over and cook other side.
4. Continue making crepes with remaining batter, greasing pan as necessary. Stack crepes on a plate or sheet of waxed paper until ready to fill.

16 crepes

Chinese Sauce

¼ cup cornstarch
4 cups chicken broth
¼ cup soy sauce
¾ cup sherry
1 teaspoon sugar

1. In a saucepan, mix cornstarch with chicken broth. Stir in remaining ingredients.
2. Cook over medium heat, stirring occasionally, until mixture thickens and comes to boiling. Remove from heat.

Chicken and Ham en Crème

¼ cup butter or margarine
¼ cup flour
½ teaspoon salt
⅛ teaspoon white pepper
½ teaspoon dry mustard
1 cup chicken broth
1½ cups cream
2 egg yolks, slightly beaten
1 cup cooked ham pieces
1½ cups cooked chicken or turkey pieces
¾ teaspoon grated lemon peel

1. Heat butter in a large saucepan over low heat. Blend in a mixture of the flour, salt, pepper, and dry mustard. Heat until bubbly.
2. Gradually add chicken broth and cream, stirring constantly. Bring to boiling, stir and cook 1 to 2 minutes.
3. Vigorously stir about 3 tablespoons of the hot mixture into the egg yolks. Immediately blend into mixture in saucepan, stirring constantly. Cook and stir 2 to 3 minutes. Mix in ham, chicken, and lemon peel.
4. Turn mixture into cooking pan of a chafing dish. Place over simmering water and heat thoroughly (do not boil).

About 6 servings

Chicken and Ham Almond: Follow recipe for Chicken and Ham en Crème. Omit lemon peel. Add ¾ **cup salted almonds.**

Creamed Chicken and Ham with Olives: Follow recipe for Chicken and Ham en Creme. Add ¾ **cup coarsely chopped ripe olives** with chicken and ham.

Chicken à la King with Ham Rolls

⅓ cup butter or margarine
⅓ cup flour
1 cup chicken broth
1 cup milk
½ teaspoon salt
⅛ teaspoon pepper
1 teaspoon grated onion
1½ cups large-diced cooked chicken
¼ cup diced green pepper
1 pimento, diced
1 can (4 ounces) sliced mushrooms (liquid included)
2 tablespoons dry sherry (optional)
6 slices boiled ham
12 cooked asparagus tips

1. Melt butter in a saucepan; add flour and stir over medium heat until bubbly. Stir in broth and milk. Cook, stirring constantly, until thickened and smooth.
2. Stir in next seven ingredients and heat thoroughly. Stir in wine, if desired.
3. Roll two asparagus tips in each ham slice. Place in cooking pan of a chafing dish. Spoon chicken à la king over ham rolls and cover pan.
4. Place over simmering water until thoroughly heated.

About 6 servings

Chicken Rissoles Deluxe

Pie crust mix for a 2-crust pie
¼ cup butter or margarine, chilled
3 tablespoons flour
Few grains pepper
2 tablespoons butter or margarine
½ cup milk
½ cup chicken broth
1 tablespoon snipped parsley
2 teaspoons grated onion
2 teaspoons drained capers
½ teaspoon crushed rosemary
½ teaspoon Worcestershire sauce
1½ cups finely chopped cooked chicken
¼ cup finely chopped cooked canned mushrooms
¼ cup finely chopped salted almonds
Oil for deep frying

1. Prepare pie crust mix according to package directions. Roll pastry ¼ inch thick on a lightly floured surface. Dot with 2 tablespoons chilled butter. Fold two sides to center and press slightly to flatten. Fold ends to center and seal edges. Wrap in plastic wrap and chill thoroughly. Roll pastry ¼ inch thick. Dot with the remaining butter. Fold, wrap, and chill thoroughly.
2. Meanwhile, add flour and pepper to the 2 tablespoons butter in a saucepan. Heat until bubbly. Gradually add milk and chicken broth, stirring constantly. Bring to boiling; cook 1 to 2 minutes.
3. Remove from heat and mix in parsley, onion, capers, rosemary, Worcestershire sauce, chicken, mushrooms, and almonds; set aside.
4. Roll out pastry about ⅛ inch thick and cut, using a cardboard pattern and a pastry wheel, into sixteen 4-inch rounds. Spoon about ¼ cup filling onto half the rounds; spread into an even layer leaving about a ½-inch border of pastry. Moisten pastry edges, cover with remaining rounds, and press with a fork to seal completely.
5. Slowly heat oil to 375°F in a wok. Fry filled rounds in the hot oil about 3 minutes, or until golden brown. Remove from oil, using a large slotted turner. Garnish each rissole with a **cherry tomato** on a pick and sprigs of **watercress**.

8 rissoles

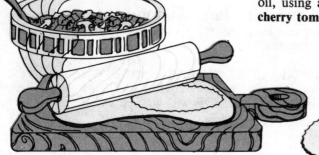

Chinese Chicken and Walnuts

2 tablespoons cooking oil
1 medium onion, thinly sliced
1 green pepper, cut in strips
2 to 3 cups coarsely chopped cooked chicken or turkey
1 can (4 ounces) mushrooms, drained (reserve liquid)
1 cup sliced celery
2 tablespoons cornstarch
1 can (13¾ ounces) chicken broth
½ cup dry white wine
Pinch white pepper
2 to 3 tablespoons Japanese soy sauce
1 cup toasted walnut pieces

1. Heat oil in a large wok. Add onion and green pepper and cook 1 to 2 minutes, stirring occasionally.
2. Stir in chicken and mushrooms. Cook slowly about 10 minutes.
3. Add celery. Mix cornstarch with ¼ cup chicken broth; set aside. Add remaining broth, wine, and mushroom liquid to chicken mixture. When liquid is hot, stir in cornstarch mixture and cook, stirring gently, until sauce is bubbling and looks clear.
4. Add pepper and soy sauce. Cook slowly 5 to 10 minutes more, or until sauce is slightly thickened. Stir in toasted walnuts.
5. Serve with **hot fluffy rice**.

6 servings

Turkey Royal

¼ cup butter or margarine
1 tablespoon minced onion
6 tablespoons flour
1 teaspoon salt
Few grains cayenne pepper
Few grains nutmeg
2 cans (4 ounces each) button
   mushrooms
Milk
3 egg yolks, slightly beaten
2 cups dairy sour cream
1 tablespoon minced parsley
1 tablespoon minced chives
¼ cup pimento strips
½ cup cooked peas
2 cups cooked turkey pieces

1. Heat butter in cooking pan of a chafing dish. Add onion and cook over low heat, stirring occasionally, until onion is transparent.
2. Blend in flour, salt, cayenne, and nutmeg. Heat until bubbly. Drain mushrooms and add enough milk to mushroom liquid to make 1 cup liquid.
3. Remove cooking pan from heat and gradually add liquid, stirring constantly. Return to heat and cook over low heat until mixture thickens, stirring constantly. Cook 1 to 2 minutes longer; remove from heat.
4. Vigorously stir about 3 tablespoons of the hot mixture into the egg yolks. Immediately blend into mixture in cooking pan. Cook over simmering water 5 to 10 minutes, or until thoroughly heated. Stir slowly to keep mixture cooking evenly. Remove from heat.
5. Using a French whip, wire whisk, or fork, vigorously stir sour cream, a little at a time, into hot mixture. Mix in parsley, chives, pimento strips, peas, mushrooms, and turkey.
6. Cook over simmering water, stirring constantly, 3 to 5 minutes, or until thoroughly heated.

6 servings

Chicken Royal: Follow recipe for Turkey Royal, substituting **cooked chicken** for the turkey.

Turkey in Buns

¾ cup ketchup
1 cup currant jelly
¼ cup finely chopped onion
2 tablespoons Worcestershire
   sauce
1 teaspoon salt
¼ teaspoon garlic salt
3 cups diced cooked turkey

1. Combine ketchup, jelly, onion, Worcestershire sauce, salt, and garlic salt in cooking pan of a chafing dish. Simmer about 20 minutes, stirring occasionally.
2. Stir in turkey. Heat over simmering water. Spoon onto **toasted buttered buns.**

8 to 10 servings

Turkey Curry

1 cup sliced fresh mushrooms
⅓ cup minced onion
1 large apple, pared and diced
3 cups diced cooked turkey
6 tablespoons butter or margarine
3 tablespoons flour
½ teaspoon salt
1 to 1½ teaspoons curry powder
1½ cups cream, or equal parts cream
   and turkey or chicken stock

1. In cooking pan of a chafing dish cook mushrooms, onion, apple, and turkey until apple and onion are tender (about 15 minutes).
2. Blend in flour, salt, and curry powder. Add liquid and cook until thickened, stirring constantly.
3. Place over hot water and cook 15 to 20 minutes, or until heated through.
4. Serve over **hot fluffy rice.**

6 servings

Pineapple Duck

1 duckling (about 3 pounds)
2 cups boiling water
  Salt and pepper
2 tablespoons soy sauce
1 can (20 ounces) pineapple
    chunks

1. Cut duckling into serving portions. Place in a large wok and cover with boiling water. Simmer, covered, until almost tender (about 1 hour).
2. Skim off fat. Stir in salt, pepper, soy sauce, and pineapple with syrup.
3. Cook 30 minutes, or until duckling is done.

4 servings

Duckling, Southern Style

2 tablespoons butter
1 tablespoon flour
2 tablespoons chopped ham
¾ teaspoon salt
⅛ teaspoon pepper
  Paprika
2 tablespoons minced onion
½ cup chopped celery
2 tablespoons chopped green
    pepper
1 tablespoon chopped parsley
1½ cups bouillon or consommé
1 whole clove
¼ teaspoon mace
2 cups diced cooked duckling

1. Melt butter in cooking pan of a chafing dish. Stir in flour and ham. Blend in salt, pepper, paprika, onion, celery, green pepper, and parsley.
2. Gradually stir in bouillon; add clove and mace. Simmer 15 minutes.
3. Stir in cooked duck and place over simmering water. Heat thoroughly and serve with **fried hominy** or **mush**.

4 servings

Goose Oriental

3 cups cooked goose meat, cut
    into 2-inch pieces
1½ cups canned pineapple juice
3 tablespoons lemon juice
¼ cup cornstarch
½ cup water
1 clove garlic, put through a
    garlic press
2 tablespoons cooking oil
1½ teaspoons salt
1 tablespoon brown sugar
½ teaspoon ginger
¼ teaspoon pepper
½ teaspoon allspice
½ teaspoon cinnamon
½ teaspoon cloves
½ teaspoon nutmeg
2 medium oranges, peeled and
    cut in segments

1. Place goose meat in a 1½-quart dish. Combine all remaining ingredients except orange segments and pour over goose. Cover and chill 2 to 3 hours.
2. Turn mixture into a large wok and cover. Bring to boiling and simmer 20 minutes, or until thoroughly heated. During last 5 minutes of cooking, place orange sections over goose; cover.
3. Serve with **hot fluffy rice** and pass bowls of **salted peanuts** and **fresh flaked coconut**.

6 servings

FISH AND SHELLFISH

Fish Balls (Fiskekroketer)

2 tablespoons butter
¼ cup sifted flour
1 teaspoon salt
⅛ teaspoon pepper
1 cup cream
3 cups flaked cooked fish (cod, trout, fillet of sole, whitefish)
1 egg yolk, beaten
2 eggs, slightly beaten
1 cup fine dry bread crumbs
Oil for deep frying

1. Melt butter in a saucepan over low heat. Blend in flour, salt, and pepper. Heat until mixture is bubbly. Add cream gradually, stirring constantly.
2. Cook rapidly, stirring constantly, until mixture thickens. Remove from heat and cool.
3. When sauce is cool, blend in flaked fish and beaten egg yolk. Shape the mixture into balls 1 inch in diameter. Dip balls into slightly beaten eggs, then coat evenly by rolling in bread crumbs.
4. Slowly heat oil to 350°F in a wok. Deep-fry as many fish balls at one time as will float uncrowded in one layer in the oil. Deep-fry 2 minutes, or until lightly browned, turning often. Drain and remove to absorbent paper.

About 5 dozen fish balls

Golden Noodles with Tuna

1 can (10½ ounces) condensed cream of mushroom soup
½ cup milk
¼ teaspoon rosemary
1 can (6½ or 7 ounces) tuna, drained and separated into large pieces
1 can (13½ ounces) pineapple tidbits, drained
½ cup salted cashew nuts
4 ounces medium noodles, cooked and drained

1. Combine soup, milk, and rosemary in a wok. Stirring frequently, bring mixture almost to boiling over medium heat.
2. Mix in tuna and pineapple, heat thoroughly, stirring occasionally.
3. Remove from heat and mix in cashew nuts. Serve over the hot noodles.

4 servings

Pineapple Trout

4 trout (about 6 ounces each)
1 lemon, cut in half
2 tablespoons flour
¼ teaspoon salt
Pinch pepper
2 to 3 tablespoons cooking oil
3 tablespoons finely sliced green onions (including tops)
5 tablespoons sugar
1½ tablespoons cornstarch
½ teaspoon ground ginger
1 can (13½ ounces) pineapple chunks, drained (reserve syrup)
¼ cup wine vinegar
1 tablespoon soy sauce
½ teaspoon bead molasses

1. Remove fins and heads from trout; rinse fish under running cold water and pat dry with absorbent paper. Rub inside of fish with lemon. Coat fish with a mixture of the flour, salt, and pepper.
2. Fry the trout in hot oil in a wok over medium heat until golden brown on one side. Turn and cook until browned on other side and fish flakes easily; sprinkle green onion over fish the last 2 or 3 minutes of cooking.
3. Transfer to a serving platter and keep warm. If desired, remove bones from fish.
4. Pour out any oil remaining in wok. Combine sugar, cornstarch, and ginger in wok. Stir in the reserved pineapple syrup plus enough water to make 1⅓ cups, the vinegar, soy sauce, and molasses. Bring rapidly to boiling; boil 2 to 3 minutes, stirring constantly. Stir in the pineapple chunks. Spoon over the fish and serve immediately.

4 servings

Sweet and Sour Fish

1 bass or other firm white fish
    (about 1½ pounds), cleaned
    and dressed with tail left on
½ cup flour
2 medium carrots, pared and cut
    diagonally into ⅛-inch
    slices
    Oil for deep-frying
2 green onions (including tops),
    sliced diagonally into ¼-inch
    pieces
¼ teaspoon ground ginger
2 medium green peppers, cleaned
    and cut in thin strips
4 large mushrooms, thinly sliced
½ teaspoon salt
5 tablespoons sugar
5 tablespoons cider vinegar
2 tablespoons Japanese soy sauce
1 tablespoon dry sherry
2 tablespoons cornstarch
1 cup cold water

1. Rinse fish in cold water and pat dry on inside and outside. With a sharp knife or cleaver, cut off head and discard. Lay the fish on its side and split in half along the backbone, removing backbone but not the tail.
2. Make three or four diagonal cuts on each side of the fish on the inside, not the skin side. Coat the fish with flour on inside and outside. Shake off excess.
3. Place carrot slices in boiling salted water. Bring to rapid boil and cook 2 to 3 minutes. Remove and set aside to drain.
4. Heat oil in a large wok to 375°F. Lower the fish into hot oil by holding it by its tail, keeping fish open and almost flat. Deep-fry 5 to 8 minutes, or until it is golden. Lift the fish out of the oil and drain on absorbent paper toweling. Keep fish warm while making sauce.
5. Remove all but 2 tablespoons oil from wok. Stir in green onion tossed with ginger, stir-frying a minute or two. Add carrots, green pepper, and mushrooms; stir-fry 2 to 3 minutes.
6. Add salt, sugar, vinegar, soy sauce, and sherry. Combine cornstarch with water and stir into mixture in wok. Cook, stirring, until sauce is thickened and vegetables are glazed.
7. Place fish on a warm platter, pour sauce over fish, and serve.

3 or 4 servings

Salmon Rabbit

4 ounces sharp Cheddar cheese,
    shredded (about 1 cup)
1 cup tomato purée
½ teaspoon salt
1 teaspoon prepared mustard
1 tablespoon Worcestershire sauce
2 eggs, slightly beaten
1 cup evaporated milk
1 can (16 ounces) salmon, drained

1. In cooking pan of a chafing dish, melt cheese over simmering water. Gradually blend in tomato purée, salt, mustard, and Worcestershire sauce, stirring constantly.
2. Combine eggs with milk and slowly stir into cheese mixture. Add salmon, separated into large chunks, and heat thoroughly. Serve on **hot buttered toast.**

6 servings

Steamed Fish Slices

1 pound frozen sole or turbot
    fillets, thawed
3 green onions including tops,
    sliced
½ teaspoon minced ginger root
8 medium mushrooms, thinly
    sliced
1 tablespoon cider vinegar
1 tablespoon soy sauce
1 tablespoon cooking oil
¼ teaspoon sugar
    Generous dash pepper

1. Place fish fillets on a plate, skin side down, so that they fit in a large wok. Scatter onion, ginger root, and mushrooms over fish.
2. Combine remaining ingredients and pour over fish and vegetables.
3. Steam fish 10 minutes, or until fish flakes easily (see steaming instructions, page 7), and serve immediately.

2 or 3 servings

Tuna Supreme

⅔ cup chopped onion
1 green pepper, cut into slivers
2 tablespoons cooking oil
1 can (10¾ ounces) condensed tomato soup
2 teaspoons soy sauce
2 to 3 tablespoons brown sugar
1 teaspoon grated lemon peel
3 tablespoons lemon juice
2 cans (6½ or 7 ounces each) tuna, drained

1. Cook onion and green pepper until almost tender in hot oil in cooking pan of a large chafing dish; stir occasionally.
2. Mix in condensed tomato soup, soy sauce, brown sugar, and lemon peel and juice. Bring to boiling; simmer 5 minutes.
3. Mix in tuna, separating it into small pieces. Cover and heat thoroughly over simmering water.
4. Serve with **hot fluffy rice.** Garnish with **toasted sesame seed** and **chow mein noodles.**

About 6 servings

Tempting Tuna Patties

2 cups soft bread crumbs
2 tablespoons lime juice
2 tablespoons water
1 can (6½ or 7 ounces) tuna, drained and flaked
1 egg, slightly beaten
¼ cup minced onion
¼ cup shredded Cheddar cheese
1 teaspoon grated Parmesan cheese
½ teaspoon salt
⅛ teaspoon pepper
2 tablespoons butter or margarine

1. Toss crumbs with a mixture of lime juice and water in a bowl.
2. In another bowl, toss the tuna with remaining ingredients, except the butter. Mix with the crumbs.
3. Heat ½ tablespoon butter in a wok. Divide tuna mixture into 4 portions, about ½ cup each, and drop 1 portion into the hot butter. Cook over medium heat, shaping into a patty as it begins to brown. Turn and brown on second side. Push up on side of wok and cook remaining patties, one at a time.
4. Serve immediately, garnished with sprigs of **parsley** and **ripe** or **pimento-stuffed olives.**

4 servings

Tuna Sukiyaki

2 tablespoons cooking oil
1 cup julienned carrots (about 2 inches long)
1 cup diagonally sliced green onion
1 cup diagonally sliced celery
2 cans (9¼ ounces each) chunk white tuna packed in water, drained and broken into chunks
1 can (8½ ounces) bamboo shoots, drained
½ cup dry sherry
1 onion bouillon cube
½ cup hot water
¼ pound fresh spinach, washed, trimmed, and cut into strips

1. Heat oil in a large wok. Add carrots and stir-fry until lightly browned. Push up on sides of wok. Add onion and celery and stir-fry until crisp-tender. Push up on sides of wok.
2. In middle of wok, mix tuna, bamboo shoots, sherry, and bouillon cube dissolved in the hot water. Simmer, uncovered, 3 minutes. Stir in spinach and simmer, covered, 2 minutes longer.
3. Serve over **hot fluffy rice.**

6 to 8 servings

Fried Clams

1 **quart fresh clams, shucked**
2 **eggs, beaten**
2 **tablespoons milk**
2 **teaspoons salt**
   Few grains pepper
3 **cups dry bread crumbs**
   Oil for deep frying

1. Drain clams and set aside.
2. Combine egg, milk, salt, and pepper. Dip clams in egg mixture and roll in bread crumbs.
3. Heat oil to 350ºF in a wok. Fry a few clams at a time in the hot oil 1 to 2 minutes, or until brown. Drain on absorbent paper.
4. Serve hot with **tartar sauce.**

About 6 servings

Crab Ravigote

¼ **cup butter**
¼ **cup flour**
1 **teaspoon salt**
   Few grains cayenne pepper
2 **cups milk**
⅔ **cup chopped cooked green pepper**
⅔ **cup coarsely chopped pimento**
2 **tablespoons capers**
2 **teaspoons tarragon vinegar**
2 **cups lump crab meat**
⅔ **cup Hollandaise Sauce**

1. Heat butter in cooking pan of a chafing dish; blend in flour, salt, and cayenne pepper; heat until bubbly. Gradually add milk, stirring constantly. Cook and stir until boiling; cook 1 minute.
2. Stir in remaining ingredients and heat thoroughly over simmering water.
3. Serve on **rusks.**

4 servings

Hollandaise Sauce: In the top of a double boiler, beat **2 egg yolks, 2 tablespoons cream, ¼ teaspoon salt,** and a **few grains cayenne pepper** until thick with a whisk beater. Set over hot (not boiling) water. Add **2 tablespoons lemon juice or tarragon vinegar** gradually, while beating constantly. Cook, beating constantly with the whisk beater, until sauce is consistency of thick cream. Remove double boiler from heat, leaving top in place. Beating constantly, add ½ **cup butter,** ½ teaspoon at a time, until the butter is melted and thoroughly blended in.

About 1 cup

Colby-Crab Fondue

⅓ **cup butter**
¾ **cup dry white wine**
1 **pound colby cheese, shredded (about 4 cups)**
2 **tablespoons flour**
1 **can (6½ ounces) crab meat**
⅛ **teaspoon garlic powder**
1 **teaspoon salt**
⅛ **teaspoon Tabasco**
1 **teaspoon prepared mustard**
1 **teaspoon bottled steak sauce**
1½ **teaspoons Worcestershire sauce**

1. Melt butter in a nonmetal fondue pot. Stir in wine and heat until bubbles appear around the edges.
2. Toss cheese with flour and stir into the hot mixture, a handful at a time. Heat and stir until completely melted.
3. Rinse, drain, and flake crab meat. Stir into cheese mixture with remaining ingredients. Heat thoroughly, stirring occasionally.
4. To serve, dip cubes of **French bread** in the warm fondue.

4 servings

Creamed Crab Meat and Mushrooms

1 can (6½ ounces) crab meat
  (about 1⅓ cups, drained)
½ pound mushrooms
  Milk
5 tablespoons butter or margarine
1 tablespoon minced onion
1 tablespoon chopped chives
1 tablespoon chopped parsley
6 tablespoons flour
1 teaspoon salt
  Few grains cayenne pepper
  Few grains nutmeg
3 egg yolks, slightly beaten
2 cups dairy sour cream
¼ cup sherry
6 Croustades

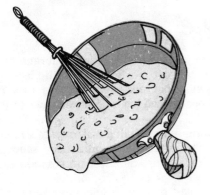

1. Remove and discard bony tissue from crab and set aside to drain.
2. Remove stems from mushroom caps. Slice both stems and caps. Set caps aside. Place stems in a small saucepan and pour in just enough cold water to barely cover the sliced stems.
3. Slowly bring to boiling, reduce heat and simmer 15 minutes. Remove from heat and drain stems, reserving liquid. Add enough milk to liquid to make 1 cup; set aside.
4. Melt butter in cooking pan of a chafing dish. Add sliced mushroom caps, drained mushroom stems, onion, chives, and parsley. Cook over medium heat until mushrooms are lightly browned and tender; stir occasionally. Remove vegetables with a slotted spoon and set aside.
5. Blend flour, salt, cayenne pepper, and nutmeg into butter in cooking pan. Heat until mixture bubbles; remove from heat.
6. Add mushroom liquid mixture gradually while stirring constantly. Return to heat and cook, stirring constantly, until mixture thickens. Cook 1 to 2 minutes longer and remove from heat.
7. Vigorously stir about 3 tablespoons of the hot mixture into the egg yolks. Immediately return to cooking pan and place over simmering water. Cook 3 to 5 minutes, stirring slowly to keep mixture cooking evenly.
8. Add the crab meat and vegetable mixture. Stirring occasionally, cook 10 to 12 minutes, or until thoroughly heated. Remove from heat.
9. Stirring vigorously with a French whip, wire whisk, or fork, add sour cream to sauce in small amounts. Stir in sherry.
10. Serve over Croustades immediately.

6 servings

Croustades

1 loaf dry bread, unsliced
  Melted butter or margarine

1. Cut bread loaf into 1¼ to 2-inch thick slices. Remove crusts and cut bread into desired shapes (see Note).
2. Brush outside and inside surfaces of shells with melted butter and place on a baking sheet.
3. Bake at 325°F 12 to 20 minutes, or until lightly browned and crisp. If shells are not to be used immediately, reheat in oven for a few minutes before filling.

6 croustades

Note: Bread slices may be cut into triangles, squares, or diamonds; or cut into rounds or fancy shapes with a large biscuit or cookie cutter. (If cutter is not deep enough, mark with it and finish cutting with the point of a sharp knife.) Following outline of shaped piece, carefully cut out center ¼ to ½ inch from edge, and down to within ¼ to ½ inch of bottom, leaving a neatly cut shell.

Lobster Newburg

¼ cup butter or margarine
2 cups cream
¾ teaspoon salt
⅛ teaspoon pepper
⅛ teaspoon nutmeg
2 cups cooked lobster meat
(1-inch pieces)
4 egg yolks, slightly beaten
2 tablespoons sherry

1. Melt butter in cooking pan of a chafing dish. Blend in cream, salt, pepper, and nutmeg. Bring just to boiling. Stir in lobster and cook over low heat until lobster is thoroughly heated.
2. Vigorously stir about 3 tablespoons of the hot mixture into the egg yolks. Immediately blend into hot mixture. Place over simmering water and cook 3 to 5 minutes, or just until mixture thickens. Stir slowly to keep mixture cooking evenly. (Do not overcook as sauce will curdle.) Remove immediately from heat.
3. Blend in sherry and serve on **toast points** or over **hot fluffy rice.**

About 6 servings

Crab Meat Newburg: Follow recipe for Lobster Newburg. Substitute **2 cups cooked crab meat** for the lobster. Remove and discard bony tissue from meat.

Rock Lobster, Cantonese Style

6 South African rock lobster tails
(3 to 5 ounces each), thawed
Lime butter*
2 cups shredded cabbage
1½ cups diagonally sliced celery
1 cup thawed frozen or fresh
peas
6 green onions, cut into ½-inch
pieces
4 carrots, cut into thin diagonal
slices
3 to 4 tablespoons cooking oil
1 cup vegetable broth
¼ cup soy sauce
1 teaspoon monosodium glutamate
1 teaspoon sugar

1. Using scissors, cut away the thin underside membrane of lobster tails. Remove meat and cut into ½- to ¾-inch pieces.
2. Cook lobster pieces slowly in hot lime butter in a large wok 5 minutes, or until lobster is opaque and tender. Set aside and keep warm.
3. Cook vegetables 5 minutes in hot oil in a wok over medium heat, stirring frequently. Stir in vegetable broth, soy sauce, monosodium glutamate, and sugar. Simmer, uncovered, 10 minutes.
4. Toss lobster with vegetables; serve with **hot fluffy rice.**

6 to 8 servings

*Blend desired amount of lime juice with melted butter.

Oyster-Potato Fries

¼ cup dairy sour cream
¼ cup flour
½ teaspoon salt
½ teaspoon seasoned salt
1 egg, beaten
2 cups finely shredded potatoes,
drained
1 pint oysters, well drained
Oil for deep frying

1. Stir sour cream and a mixture of flour, salt, and seasoned salt into beaten egg. Combine with potatoes and blend thoroughly. Add oysters to potato mixture.
2. Slowly heat oil to 365°F in a wok.
3. Drop mixture by tablespoonfuls with an oyster in each spoonful into the hot oil. Do not crowd the oysters; they should be free to float one layer deep. Fry 2 to 3 minutes, or until golden brown.
4. Remove with a slotted spoon and drain over oil before removing to absorbent paper.

About 30

Creamed Oysters and Turkey

6 tablespoons butter or margarine
6 tablespoons flour
¾ teaspoon salt
¼ teaspoon pepper
3 cups milk or cream
1 can (2¼ ounces) deviled ham
3 cups cooked turkey pieces
½ pint oysters (shell particles removed)
8 toast cups

1. Heat butter in cooking pan of a chafing dish over direct heat. Blend in flour, salt, and pepper. Heat until mixture bubbles, stirring constantly.
2. Gradually add milk, stirring constantly; cook 1 to 2 minutes longer. Mix in the deviled ham, turkey, and oysters. Heat thoroughly, stirring occasionally. Keep hot over simmering water, if necessary.
3. Fill toast cups with creamed mixture. Serve immediately.

8 servings

Toast cups: To make 8 toast cups, cut crusts from **8 thin bread slices.** Lightly brush both sides with **melted butter or margarine** and press each slice into a muffin pan well, corners pointing up. Toast in a 325°F oven 12 to 20 minutes, or until crisp and lightly browned.

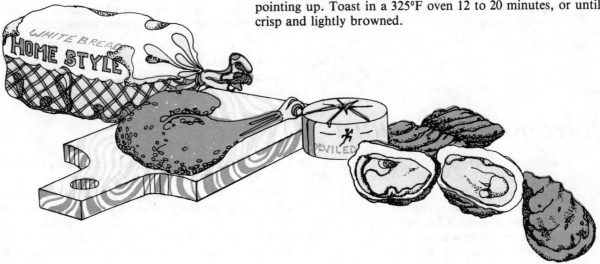

Oysters à la Newburg

1 pint oysters
1 teaspoon water
½ teaspoon dry mustard
¼ cup butter or margarine
2 tablespoons flour
1 teaspoon salt
⅛ teaspoon nutmeg
⅛ teaspoon pepper
2 cups half-and-half
¼ teaspoon Worcestershire sauce
4 egg yolks, slightly beaten
2 tablespoons sherry

1. Heat oysters in their own liquor just until edges curl. Drain; set aside and keep warm. Blend water with dry mustard and set aside.
2. Heat butter in top of a double boiler over direct heat. Blend in flour, salt, nutmeg, and pepper. Heat until mixture is bubbly. Remove from heat.
3. Gradually add half-and-half and Worcestershire sauce, stirring constantly. Blend mustard mixture into sauce. Bring rapidly to boiling over direct heat, stirring constantly. Cook 1 to 2 minutes longer.
4. Vigorously stir about 3 tablespoons of the hot mixture into the egg yolks. Immediately blend into mixture in top of double boiler and place over simmering water. Cook 3 to 5 minutes, stirring slowly to keep mixture cooking evenly. Remove from heat.
5. Blend in sherry; add oysters and turn into cooking pan of a chafing dish. Keep warm over simmering water and serve on crisp toast.

6 servings

Oysters Royale

6 tablespoons butter
½ clove garlic, minced
½ cup diced celery
½ cup diced green pepper
6 or 7 tablespoons flour
½ teaspoon salt
¼ teaspoon white pepper
Few grains cayenne pepper
2 cups half-and-half
1½ pints oysters, drained
    (reserve ⅓ cup liquor)*
1 teaspoon prepared mustard
2 ounces Gruyère cheese, cut into
    pieces
¼ cup dry sherry

1. Heat butter in a saucepan. Add garlic, celery, and green pepper; cook about 5 minutes, or until vegetables are crisp-tender. Remove vegetables with a slotted spoon and set aside.
2. Blend a mixture of flour, salt, and peppers, into butter in saucepan; heat until mixture bubbles. Remove from heat; add half-and-half and reserved oyster liquor gradually, stirring constantly. Continue stirring, bring to boiling, and boil 1 to 2 minutes. Remove from heat.
3. Blend in mustard and cheese, stirring until cheese is melted. Mix in wine, vegetables, and oysters. Bring just to boiling and remove from heat. (Edges of oysters should just begin to curl.) Turn into cooking pan of a chafing dish and set over simmering water.
4. Accompany with a basket of **toasted buttered 3½-inch bread rounds** sprinkled lightly with **ground nutmeg.**

10 to 12 servings

*The amount of liquor in a pint of oysters varies; using slightly less than ⅓ cup will not affect the recipe.

Neapolitan Shrimp

3 tablespoons olive or other
    cooking oil
2 cloves garlic, minced
2 pounds cleaned and shelled
    shrimp (thawed if frozen)
8 anchovies, cut into pieces
2 cans (16 ounces each) tomatoes,
    forced through a food mill
8 pimento-stuffed olives, sliced
8 pitted ripe olives, sliced
2 teaspoons capers
1 teaspoon dried basil
⅛ teaspoon Tabasco
¼ teaspoon sugar

1. In cooking pan of a chafing dish, heat oil. Add garlic and cook over low heat until tender but not browned.
2. Stir in shrimp. Cook until shrimp turns pink and flesh is firm (about 5 minutes). Remove shrimp from pan and set aside.
3. Add anchovies to liquid in cooking pan; cook 1 minute. Add tomatoes and simmer over low heat 10 minutes. Add olives, capers, basil, Tabasco, and sugar. Cook, uncovered, 15 minutes.
4. Add shrimp to sauce and heat 10 minutes. Keep warm over simmering water. Serve over **hot fluffy rice.**

6 servings

Shrimp Meunière

1½ pounds uncooked shrimp, shelled
½ cup butter
1 tablespoon lime juice
¼ teaspoon salt
⅛ teaspoon freshly ground
    black pepper
1 teaspoon minced fresh
    parsley

1. Wash shelled shrimp and pat dry. Melt butter in cooking pan of a chafing dish. Stir in the shrimp and cook, turning often, until lightly browned (about 10 minutes).
2. Using a slotted spoon, remove shrimp to a warm platter. Add lime juice, salt, and pepper to butter in pan. Heat thoroughly, return the shrimp to the cooking pan, and coat with the butter sauce.
3. Sprinkle parsley over top and serve shrimp with **hot fluffy rice.**

4 to 6 servings

Shrimp Aphrodite

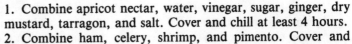

1 can (12 ounces) apricot
    nectar
1¼ cups water
2 tablespoons cider vinegar
2 tablespoons sugar
½ teaspoon ground ginger
½ teaspoon dry mustard
½ teaspoon dried tarragon
¼ teaspoon salt
5 cups julienned cooked ham
1½ cups thinly sliced celery
2 cups cooked shrimp, halved
    lengthwise
1 jar (4 ounces) pimentos,
    cut into strips
3 tablespoons butter
¾ cup thinly sliced white
    onion
1½ tablespoons cornstarch
3 tablespoons lime juice

1. Combine apricot nectar, water, vinegar, sugar, ginger, dry mustard, tarragon, and salt. Cover and chill at least 4 hours.
2. Combine ham, celery, shrimp, and pimento. Cover and chill.
3. When ready to serve, melt butter in cooking pan of a chafing dish. Sauté the onion until soft but not brown. Stir in the chilled apricot mixture; cover and simmer 10 minutes.
4. Stir in the chilled ham, celery, shrimp, and pimento. Cover and simmer 10 minutes. Blend cornstarch with lime juice. Stir carefully into mixture until sauce bubbles. Cook 1 to 2 minutes, stirring constantly. Serve over **hot fluffy rice.**

6 to 8 servings

Shrimp Jambalaya

2 to 3 tablespoons cooking oil
½ cup chopped onion
½ cup chopped green onion
½ cup chopped green pepper
½ cup chopped celery
¼ pound diced cooked ham
2 cloves garlic, minced
2 cups chicken broth
3 large tomatoes, coarsely
    chopped
¼ cup chopped parsley
½ teaspoon salt
⅛ teaspoon pepper
¼ teaspoon thyme
⅛ teaspoon cayenne pepper
1 bay leaf
1 cup uncooked rice
3 cans (4½ ounces each) shrimp,
    rinsed under running cold
    water
¼ cup coarsely chopped green
    pepper

1. Heat oil in a large wok over low heat. Stir in onion, green onion, green pepper, celery, ham, and garlic. Cook over medium heat about 5 minutes, or until onion is tender, stirring occasionally.
2. Stir in chicken broth, tomatoes, parsley, salt, pepper, thyme, cayenne pepper, and bay leaf; cover and bring to boiling.
3. Add rice gradually, stirring with a fork. Simmer, covered, 20 minutes, or until rice is tender.
4. Mix in shrimp and remaining green pepper. Simmer, uncovered, about 5 minutes longer.

6 to 8 servings

Shrimp Creole

¼ cup butter or margarine
½ cup chopped onion
½ cup chopped celery
⅓ cup chopped green pepper
3 tablespoons flour
1 can (16 ounces) tomatoes, sieved
1 bay leaf
1 large sprig parsley
1½ teaspoons salt
1 teaspoon sugar
¾ teaspoon Worcestershire sauce
¼ teaspoon freshly ground black pepper
2 or 3 drops Tabasco
¾ pound cooked shrimp

1. Heat butter in cooking pan of a chafing dish. Add onion, celery, and green pepper. Cook over medium heat, stirring occasionally, until onion is transparent and other vegetables are tender.
2. Blend in flour and heat until mixture is bubbly. Gradually stir in remaining ingredients except shrimp.
3. Simmer sauce, covered, 30 minutes. Remove bay leaf and parsley. Stir in shrimp and cook over simmering water until thoroughly heated. Serve over **hot fluffy rice.**

4 or 5 servings

Shrimp in Sour Cream Sauce

¼ cup butter or margarine
2 tablespoons olive oil
1 cup chopped scallions or green onions
1 pound fresh mushrooms, sliced
¼ cup finely chopped parsley
¼ cup Madeira
1½ pounds fresh shrimp, peeled, deveined, rinsed, and drained
½ to 1 teaspoon salt
⅛ teaspoon black pepper
1 cup dairy sour cream

1. Heat butter and olive oil in cooking pan of a chafing dish over direct heat. Add scallions and cook 2 minutes. Add mushrooms and cook 5 minutes. Mix in parsley and wine. Add shrimp and cook until they turn pink. Season with salt and pepper.
2. Remove from heat. Blend in sour cream and heat (*do not boil*). Sprinkle with an additional 2 teaspoons wine, if desired. Place cooking pan over hot water. Serve on **toast rounds.**

About 6 servings

Shrimp and Vegetables Italian Style

¼ cup cooking oil
1 pound cleaned uncooked shrimp, thawed, rinsed, and drained well
3 medium zucchini (1 pound), sliced
1 medium onion, chopped
1 clove garlic, minced
¼ cup minced parsley
1 teaspoon dried dill weed
1 teaspoon salt
⅛ teaspoon pepper
1½ teaspoons lemon juice
¼ cup grated Romano cheese

1. Heat 2 tablespoons oil in a large wok. Add shrimp and stir-fry over high heat until cooked (about 3 minutes). Remove shrimp from wok and pour out oil.
2. Heat 2 tablespoons more oil in the wok. Stir in zucchini, onion, and garlic. Stir-fry until tender.
3. Add parsley, dill, salt, pepper, and shrimp. Cover and simmer 10 minutes.
4. Sprinkle lemon juice and cheese over mixture. Toss well and serve.

4 servings

Shrimp-Tuna Medley

1 to 2 tablespoons cooking oil
½ cup chopped onion
½ cup chopped celery
1½ pounds fresh shrimp, peeled, deveined, rinsed, and cut in halves lengthwise
1 teaspoon sugar
3 medium (about 1 pound) tomatoes, cut into large pieces
1 cup sliced water chestnuts
½ cup chopped green pepper
½ cup bottled barbecue sauce
1 can (6½ or 7 ounces) tuna, drained and flaked
1 tablespoon cornstarch
¾ cup water
2 cups packaged precooked rice, prepared according to package directions
1 tablespoon butter or margarine
2 tablespoons snipped parsley

1. Heat cooking oil in a large wok; add onion and celery and cook until soft.
2. Add shrimp and stir-fry about 5 minutes, or until shrimp turns pink.
3. Sprinkle sugar over tomatoes. Blend tomatoes, water chestnuts, green pepper, barbecue sauce, and tuna into the shrimp mixture; cook 5 minutes, stirring occasionally.
4. Blend cornstarch and water; stir into shrimp mixture and bring to boiling. Reduce heat and simmer 5 minutes, stirring occasionally.
5. Gently toss rice, the 1 tablespoon butter, and parsley together. Spoon the rice around edge of a serving dish. Turn tuna-shrimp mixture into center.

6 servings

Stir-Fried Shrimp and Vegetables

¾ pound fresh bean sprouts
2 tablespoons cornstarch
2 teaspoons sugar
1½ cups water
2 tablespoons Japanese soy sauce
3 tablespoons white wine vinegar
½ teaspoon pepper
2 tablespoons sesame oil
1 teaspoon salt
1 cup diagonally sliced celery
6 green onions, sliced diagonally into 1-inch pieces
1 cup thinly sliced fresh mushrooms
1 tablespoon sesame oil
2 cloves garlic, minced
1 teaspoon minced fresh ginger root
¾ pound cleaned and cooked shrimp
1 package (6 ounces) frozen snow peas, thawed and well drained

1. Blanch bean sprouts by turning half of them into a sieve or basket and setting in a saucepan of boiling water. Boil 1 minute. Remove from water and spread out on absorbent paper to drain. Repeat with remaining bean sprouts.
2. Blend cornstarch, sugar, water, soy sauce, vinegar, and pepper; set aside.
3. Heat 2 tablespoons sesame oil in a large wok. Stir in salt, celery, green onion, and mushrooms. Stir-fry vegetables about 1 minute. Add bean sprouts and stir-fry 1 minute more. Remove vegetables from wok.
4. Heat 1 tablespoon sesame oil. Add garlic and ginger root; stir-fry briefly. Add shrimp and snow peas; stir-fry 1 minute longer. Return other vegetables to wok and mix together. Stir-fry briefly to heat.
5. Push vegetables and shrimp up sides of wok. Stir cornstarch mixture into liquid in center of wok. Cook until thickened and combine with shrimp and vegetables. Serve immediately.

4 servings

PASTA AND RICE

Chili Don Pedro

8 ounces medium noodles,
  cooked and drained
1 tablespoon butter or margarine
3 cans (about 16 ounces each)
  chili with beans
8 ounces creamed cottage cheese
1 package (8 ounces) cream
  cheese, cut into ¾-inch cubes
½ cup dairy sour cream

1. Toss cooked noodles with butter; keep warm.
2. Mix chili, cheeses, and sour cream in cooking pan of a large chafing dish. Cover and simmer until the mixture is thoroughly heated, stirring occasionally. If necessary, blend in additional sour cream until of desired consistency.
3. To serve, combine noodles with the chili mixture and sprinkle **snipped parsley** over top.

8 servings

Garlic-Buttered Noodles

½ cup butter
1 clove garlic, minced
1 teaspoon salt
¼ teaspoon pepper
8 ounces medium noodles,
  cooked and drained
1 cup bread crumbs, browned
  in butter

1. Place butter, garlic, salt, and pepper in cooking pan of a chafing dish. Heat just until butter is lightly browned.
2. Place cooking pan over simmering water. Add noodles and crumbs. Toss lightly until noodles are well coated and crumbs are evenly distributed.

About 8 servings

Noodle Omelet

1½ cups (4 ounces) noodles
3 tablespoons butter
2 tablespoons chopped onion
3 eggs
2 tablespoons milk or water
½ teaspoon salt
⅛ teaspoon pepper

1. Cook noodles according to package directions. Drain well.
2. Melt butter in a large wok over low heat. Add onion and cook until soft but not browned. Stir in noodles.
3. Meanwhile, beat eggs, milk, salt, and pepper with a fork; beat just enough to mix well. Pour over noodle mixture.
4. Cook rapidly, lifting mixture with fork, at the same time tilting wok to let uncooked egg mixture flow to bottom.
5. When mixture is set, reduce heat and cook 1 or 2 minutes longer to brown the bottom. Loosen edges and slide a spatula underneath to be sure omelet is free. Fold in half and slide out of wok onto a warm platter.

4 servings

Noodle Supper

½ pound lean ground beef
1 teaspoon salt
¼ cup chopped parsley
1 package (1½ ounces) dry
    onion soup mix
1 quart hot water
1 cup sliced carrots
4 ounces medium noodles

1. Place ground beef in a large wok. Sprinkle with salt and brown lightly, stirring frequently.
2. Stir in parsley, soup mix, water, and carrots. Bring to boiling. Reduce heat and simmer 10 to 15 minutes, stirring occasionally.
3. Stir in noodles and cover. Cook about 10 minutes, or until noodles are tender.

4 servings

Noodles with Cream and Eggs

8 ounces medium noodles
½ cup butter
¾ cup freshly grated Parmesan
    cheese
    Freshly ground black pepper
2 egg yolks, slightly beaten
½ cup whipping cream, warmed

1. Cook noodles in boiling salted water as directed on package; drain.
2. Melt butter in cooking pan of a chafing dish. Place cooking pan over simmering water, add noodles to pan, and toss gently with butter. Sprinkle on cheese and a generous amount of pepper while tossing.
3. When cheese is well mixed and noodles are coated, stir egg yolks into the noodles.
4. Toss the noodles again and add whipping cream. Toss again and serve immediately in hot soup bowls.

4 to 6 servings

Shupp Noodles

6 ounces uncooked noodles
½ cup butter
3 eggs
½ teaspoon salt
    Pinch pepper

1. Cook noodles in boiling salted water about 10 minutes. Rinse and drain well.
2. Melt butter in cooking pan of a chafing dish. Add the cooked noodles and cook over low heat until lightly browned, stirring occasionally.
3. Beat eggs with salt and pepper, and stir into the noodles. Cook over simmering water until eggs are set.

4 to 6 servings

Deep-Fried Noodles

6 ounces fine noodles
    Oil for deep frying

1. Cook noodles in boiling salted water according to package directions. Rinse with cold water, drain, separate, and place on absorbent paper to dry.
2. Heat oil in a wok to 375°F. Place about ½ cup noodles in the hot oil. Fry until golden brown, turning once.
3. Drain on absorbent paper and sprinkle with salt, if desired. If not to be used immediately, noodles may be reheated in a 400°F oven.

4 to 6 servings

Spaghetti-Cheese Pie

8 ounces spaghetti, cooked
    and drained
½ cup chopped celery
¼ cup chopped onion
1 tablespoon poppy seed
½ teaspoon salt
¼ teaspoon pepper
½ cup evaporated milk
3 tablespoons butter or margarine
8 ounces sharp Cheddar cheese,
    shredded (about 2 cups)

1. Combine spaghetti, celery, onion, poppy seed, salt, pepper, and evaporated milk in a large bowl.
2. Heat butter in cooking pan of a chafing dish. Spoon half the spaghetti mixture into the pan, spreading evenly. Sprinkle with 1½ cups cheese. Top with remaining spaghetti mixture and cheese.
3. Cover and cook over simmering water 15 to 25 minutes, running a spatula under mixture occasionally to prevent sticking.
4. Cut into six wedges and serve.

6 servings

Confetti Noodles

6 ounces fine noodles
¼ pound bacon, diced
1 tablespoon butter
¼ pound mushrooms, sliced
2 green onions (tops included),
    thinly sliced diagonally
¼ teaspoon salt
⅛ teaspoon pepper
¼ cup grated Parmesan cheese

1. Cook noodles in boiling salted water according to package directions. Rinse and drain well.
2. Meanwhile, fry bacon in a large wok until crisp. Remove bacon and pour off all drippings except 2 tablespoons.
3. Add butter to bacon drippings in wok and heat. Add mushrooms, green onions, salt, and pepper; stir-fry until mushrooms are lightly browned.
4. Stir in noodles and bacon. Turn into a serving dish and toss with cheese.

4 to 6 servings

Curried Rice

1 tablespoon cooking oil
1 cup minced onion
1 cup chopped green pepper
½ cup currants
2 cups uncooked rice
1 teaspoon salt
½ teaspoon pepper
½ teaspoon curry powder
1 quart chicken broth

1. Heat oil in a large wok. Stir in onion, green pepper, and currants. Stir-fry until tender (about 10 minutes).
2. Stir in rice and seasonings; brown slightly.
3. Pour broth over rice and mix well. Bring to boiling, cover, and simmer 20 to 25 minutes, or until rice is tender.

8 servings

Bacon-and-Egg Fried Rice

10 slices bacon
½ cup chopped onion
1 cup diagonally sliced celery
1 cup sliced mushrooms
3 cups cooked rice
2 tablespoons Japanese soy sauce
1 egg, slightly beaten

1. Cook bacon, 5 slices at a time, in a large wok until crisp. Remove bacon and pour out all but 3 tablespoons bacon drippings.
2. Stir-fry onion and celery in the hot fat until almost tender. Stir in mushrooms, rice, and soy sauce. Cook 5 minutes over low heat, stirring occasionally.
3. Stir in egg and cook only until egg is set. Turn into a serving dish. Crumble bacon over top and serve immediately.

6 servings

Fried Rice

2 tablespoons butter
¾ cup uncooked rice
2 tablespoons very finely
    chopped fresh mushrooms
½ teaspoon grated onion
3 chicken bouillon cubes
2½ cups boiling water
1 tablespoon finely chopped
    carrot
1 tablespoon finely chopped
    green pepper

1. Melt butter in a wok over low heat. Add rice, mushrooms, and onion. Cook until golden brown.
2. Dissolve bouillon cubes in boiling water and stir into rice mixture. Cover and cook over low heat 30 minutes, or until rice is tender.
3. Add carrot and green pepper; toss lightly.

About 8 servings

Rice Pancakes

1 cup cooked white rice
2 tablespoons finely chopped
    scallions or green onion
2 tablespoons finely chopped
    green pepper
2 tablespoons finely chopped
    celery
2 tablespoons finely chopped
    water chestnuts
2 eggs, slightly beaten
¼ teaspoon salt
    Dash peper
2 tablespoons cooking oil
    Foo Yong Sauce (page 32)

1. Combine all ingredients except oil and Foo Yong Sauce.
2. Heat oil in a wok. Add about a fourth of the egg-rice mixture, just enough to cover bottom of wok. Cook over low heat until eggs are set. Loosen pancake, turn over, and push up on sides of wok or remove to warm platter to keep warm while cooking remaining pancakes.
3. Cook 3 more pancakes with remaining mixture. Turn out onto a hot serving plate and serve with hot Foo Yong Sauce.

4 servings

Rice Pilaf Deluxe

1½ cups uncooked long-grain rice
⅓ cup finely chopped onion
⅓ cup butter
1½ teaspoons salt
3 cans (about 14 ounces each)
    chicken broth
¾ cup golden raisins
3 tablespoons butter
¾ cup coarsely chopped pecans
¼ teaspoon salt

1. Add rice and onion to ⅓ cup hot butter in a large wok. Stir-fry until lightly browned.
2. Stir in salt, broth, and raisins. Cover, bring to boiling, and cook over low heat about 25 minutes. Remove cover and cook 5 minutes, or until rice is tender and liquid is completely absorbed.
3. Meanwhile, heat remaining butter in a small skillet. Add pecans and ¼ teaspoon salt; heat 2 to 3 minutes, stirring occasionally.
4. Serve rice topped with buttered pecans.

8 servings

Nasi Goreng

3 to 4 tablespoons cooking oil
¾ cup chopped onion
2 cloves garlic, finely chopped
1¼ teaspoons Tabasco
¾ pound cooked chicken, chopped
1 cup cooked small shrimp
3½ cups cooked rice
¼ teaspoon salt
  Curry Pancakes
2 ounces cooked ham, cut in thin strips
2 cucumber pickles, sliced

1. Heat oil in a large wok. Add onion, garlic, and Tabasco; stir-fry until onion is tender, but not brown.
2. Mix in chicken, shrimp, rice, and salt; heat thoroughly.
3. Turn mixture onto a heated large platter. Garnish the edge with rolled pancake strips and then top with ham strips and pickle slices.

4 to 6 servings

Curry Pancakes

¼ cup all-purpose flour
⅛ teaspoon salt
⅛ teaspoon curry powder
¼ cup water
2 eggs, fork beaten

1. Mix flour, salt, and curry powder. Gradually add water, stirring well. Mix in eggs, stirring until batter is smooth.
2. Pour batter onto a preheated lightly greased griddle, forming 4-inch pancakes. Turn pancakes as they become puffy and full of bubbles. Brown on other side.
3. Roll up each pancake and cut into ¼-inch-wide strips.

Sweet Potatoes and Rice

½ cup butter or margarine
1½ cups coarsely chopped celery
1½ cups chopped onion
2 cups packaged precooked rice
3 chicken bouillon cubes
2½ cups boiling water
2 tablespoons brown sugar
1¾ teaspoons salt
½ teaspoon pepper
1 teaspoon ground coriander
¾ teaspoon crushed rosemary
¼ teaspoon ground ginger
2 eggs, slightly beaten
1 can (17 ounces) sweet potatoes, drained and cut into ½-inch pieces

1. Heat butter in a large wok. Stir in celery, onion, and rice. Cook, uncovered, until rice is golden yellow in color, stirring occasionally.
2. Dissolve bouillon cubes in boiling water and add 2 cups of the broth to rice mixture. Blend in a mixture of brown sugar and dry ingredients. Bring to boiling and cook, covered, over low heat 15 minutes, or until rice is tender.
3. Mix eggs with remaining broth. Blend into rice mixture. Add sweet potatoes; toss gently. Heat thoroughly before serving.

About 8 servings

Strawberry-Pear Fondue, 76

Artichokes in Mushroom Cream

2 packages (9 ounces each) frozen artichoke hearts
¼ cup butter
4 ounces mushrooms, coarsely chopped
2 tablespoons finely chopped onion
2½ tablespoons flour
¼ teaspoon salt
⅛ teaspoon white pepper
⅛ teaspoon ground nutmeg
¾ cup chicken broth (dissolve 1 chicken bouillon cube in ¾ cup boiling water)
¾ cup cream
2 egg yolks, slightly beaten
2 tablespoons snipped parsley
½ teaspoon capers
8 patty shells

1. Cook artichoke hearts according to package directions, substituting **seasoned salt** for salt. Drain and set aside.
2. Meanwhile, heat butter in cooking pan of a chafing dish; add mushrooms and onion. Cook, stirring occasionally, until mushrooms are lightly browned.
3. Blend in a mixture of the flour, salt, pepper, and nutmeg. Heat until bubbly. Remove from heat and add broth and cream gradually, stirring constantly; bring sauce to boiling and cook 1 to 2 minutes, stirring constantly.
4. Remove from heat and vigorously stir about 3 tablespoons of the mixture into egg yolks. Immediately return to double boiler. Cook over boiling water about 5 minutes, stirring slowly so mixture cooks evenly.
5. Mix in artichoke hearts, parsley, and capers. Heat thoroughly over simmering water.
6. Spoon mixture into warm patty shells. Replace patty shell tops or garnish with tiny fancy shapes cut from a crimson **cinnamon apple** or a **grenadine pear**.

8 servings

Broccoli with Buttery Lemon Crunch

½ cup coarse dry bread crumbs
¼ cup butter
1 tablespoon grated lemon peel
3 tablespoons butter
1 small clove garlic, minced
½ teaspoon salt
Few grains pepper
1½ pounds broccoli, cooked and drained

1. Lightly brown crumbs in ¼ cup butter in a large skillet. Remove from butter with slotted spoon and mix crumbs with lemon peel.
2. Put the 3 tablespoons butter, garlic, salt, and pepper into cooking pan of a chafing dish. Heat until butter is lightly browned. Add broccoli and turn gently until well coated with butter. Top with "lemoned" crumbs.

About 6 servings

Company Cabbage

5 cups finely shredded cabbage
1 cup finely shredded carrot
½ cup chopped green onion
½ teaspoon salt
⅛ teaspoon pepper
1 beef bouillon cube
¼ cup boiling water
¼ cup butter
1 teaspoon prepared mustard
⅓ cup chopped pecans
¼ teaspoon paprika

1. Combine cabbage, carrots, onion, salt, and pepper in a large wok.
2. Dissolve bouillon cube in boiling water and add to vegetables in wok; toss with fork to blend thoroughly. Cover tightly and cook over low heat 5 minutes; stir once during cooking. Drain if necessary. Turn into a warm serving dish. Keep hot.
3. Melt butter in a small saucepan. Stir in mustard and pecans and heat thoroughly. Pour over vegetables. Sprinkle with paprika.

6 servings

New Cabbage in Orange Sauce

2 tablespoons butter or
   margarine
2 tablespoons sugar
1½ tablespoons lemon juice
1 teaspoon grated onion
½ teaspoon salt
¼ teaspoon pepper
3 cups (about ½ pound) coarsely
   shredded new cabbage
1 orange, thinly sliced and
   quartered
½ cup orange juice

1. Melt butter in a large wok. Add sugar, lemon juice, onion, salt, pepper, cabbage, and orange slices. Stir to mix thoroughly. Pour in orange juice.
2. Simmer, stirring occasionally, until cabbage is just tender (about 3 minutes). Serve at once in individual sauce dishes.

About 6 servings

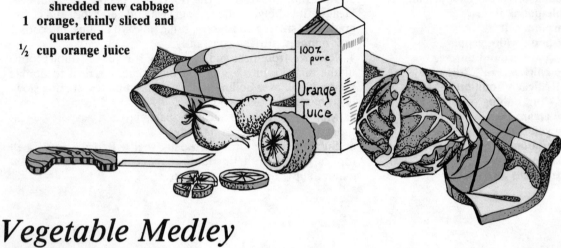

Vegetable Medley

5 cups finely shredded cabbage
1 medium onion, chopped
1 can (16 ounces) bean sprouts,
   drained
1 cup coarsely shredded carrots
½ cup green pepper strips
1 cup boiling water
1 teaspoon salt
⅛ teaspoon pepper
1 tablespoon soy sauce
1 teaspoon prepared mustard
¼ cup vegetable oil
½ cup chopped water chestnuts

1. In a large wok, mix cabbage, onion, bean sprouts, carrots, green pepper, water, salt, and pepper. Cook, closely covered, until cabbage is crisp-tender (about 5 minutes); stir several times during cooking.
2. Blend soy sauce, mustard, vegetable oil, and water chestnuts. Add to vegetables and toss lightly to blend, adding more salt if necessary.
3. Cook several minutes longer, uncovered, and serve when thoroughly heated.

8 servings

Glossy Carrots

24 small whole carrots, pared
   and cooked
¼ cup butter or margarine
¼ cup thawed frozen orange
   juice concentrate
2 teaspoons honey
½ teaspoon ground ginger
½ teaspoon salt

1. While carrots are cooking, melt butter in cooking pan of a chafing dish. Blend in orange juice concentrate, honey, and a mixture of ginger and salt.
2. Add carrots and heat over chafing dish burner, turning carrots until well glazed.

About 4 servings

Corn-Gold Fritters

1⅓ cups sifted all-purpose flour
1 teaspoon baking powder
¾ teaspoon salt
⅛ teaspoon pepper
⅔ cup milk
1 teaspoon Worcestershire sauce
1 teaspoon cooking oil
2 eggs, well beaten
1 can (12 ounces) whole kernel
    corn, drained
    Oil for deep frying

1. Blend flour, baking powder, salt, and pepper in a bowl.
2. Mix milk, Worcestershire sauce, and oil with eggs. Add all at one time to the dry ingredients and beat with a hand rotary beater just until smooth. Mix in corn.
3. Place oil in a wok and heat slowly to 365°F. Drop batter by tablespoonfuls into the hot oil until surface is covered. Fry 2 to 3 minutes, or until golden brown, turning frequently.
4. Drain fritters over oil a few seconds before removing to absorbent paper.

About 6 servings

Corn "Oysters"

1 cup sifted all-purpose flour
1 teaspoon baking powder
1 teaspoon sugar
½ teaspoon salt
¼ teaspoon paprika
2 teaspoons dill weed, crushed
2 cups fresh corn kernels cut from
    cob (about 4 ears)
6 tablespoons milk
2 egg yolks, beaten
2 egg whites
    Oil for shallow frying

1. Sift flour, baking powder, sugar, salt, and paprika together into a bowl. Stir in dill weed and a mixture of corn, milk, and beaten egg yolks. Fold in stiffly beaten egg whites.
2. Place oil in a wok and heat slowly to 365°F.
3. Drop batter by the teaspoonful into the hot oil. Fry uncrowded until golden on both sides, turning once. Lift out of oil with a slotted spoon and drain on an absorbent-paper-lined baking sheet. Serve hot.

About 6 servings

Corn with Mushrooms

2 tablespoons butter or margarine
¼ cup thinly sliced green onion
⅔ cup coarsely chopped
    mushrooms
1 can (12 ounces) whole kernel
    corn, drained
½ cup cream
½ teaspoon salt
⅛ teaspoon pepper
2 tablespoons snipped parsley

1. Melt butter in cooking pan of a chafing dish. Add onion and mushrooms and sauté 5 minutes.
2. Add corn and stir mixture gently over medium heat until thoroughly heated.
3. Add cream, salt, pepper, and parsley. Place over simmering water to keep warm until ready to serve.

4 to 6 servings

Dilled Green Beans with Cauliflower

1 package (10 ounces) frozen
    cauliflower, thawed
1 package (10 ounces) frozen cut
    green beans, thawed
2 to 3 tablespoons olive oil
2 teaspoons dill weed
1 teaspoon salt
¼ teaspoon pepper
¼ cup minced onion
¼ cup wine vinegar
¼ teaspoon dill weed

1. Cut cauliflower into flowerets and cut stems in half down the middle. Set aside with green beans to drain.
2. Heat olive oil in a large wok. Stir in dill weed, salt, pepper, and onion. Stir-fry a minute or two.
3. Add vegetables and stir-fry to coat with oil. Cover, and simmer about 4 minutes, or until vegetables are crisp-tender.
4. Toss with vinegar and dill weed. Serve immediately.

6 servings

Green Beans with Tomato

1 pound fresh green beans, cut
    diagonally into 1-inch pieces
¼ cup butter or margarine
¼ cup finely chopped onion
1 small clove garlic, crushed in
    a garlic press
1 tablespoon lemon juice
2 medium-size ripe tomatoes, cut
    into pieces
1 tablespoon brown sugar
1 teaspoon salt
⅛ teaspoon black pepper
½ teaspoon oregano

1. Cook green beans in boiling salted water until tender; drain.
2. While beans are cooking, heat butter in cooking pan of a chafing dish. Add onion and garlic and cook over medium heat 3 minutes. Add remaining ingredients and heat thoroughly, stirring occasionally.
3. Add green beans to tomato mixture; mix gently. Place over simmering water to keep warm.

6 to 8 servings

Western Lettuce and Spinach

1 small head iceberg lettuce
¾ pound fresh spinach
1 clove garlic, crushed in a
    garlic press
1 tablespoon water
1 jar (3½ ounces) whole
    mushrooms
2 tablespoons butter or margarine
2 teaspoons sugar
¼ teaspoon monosodium glutamate
¼ teaspoon salt
⅛ teaspoon nutmeg
1 tablespoon chopped pimento
1 to 2 tablespoons lemon juice
1 tablespoon cornstarch

1. Core, rinse, and drain lettuce slightly. Tear enough lettuce into large pieces to make about 2 quarts, lightly packed.
2. Remove stems from spinach, wash leaves thoroughly, and drain slightly.
3. Place lettuce and spinach in a large wok with garlic. Add water. Cover and cook over medium heat until leaves are heated through and begin to soften. Push up on sides of wok.
4. Stir mushrooms with liquid and remaining ingredients, except lemon juice and cornstarch, into liquid in wok. Bring to boiling. Combine lemon juice with cornstarch and stir into liquid. Cook and stir until boiling and thickened. Cook 1 minute longer.
5. Stir lettuce mixture into mushroom sauce and serve at once.

4 to 6 servings

French-Style Green Beans with Water Chestnuts

1 can (5 ounces) water chestnuts,
    drained, sliced, and slivered
3 tablespoons chopped onion
¼ cup butter or margarine
½ teaspoon salt
    Few grains pepper
2 tablespoons lemon juice
1 teaspoon soy sauce
1 pound fresh green beans,
    frenched, cooked, and drained

1. Brown slivered water chestnuts and onion in hot butter in a large wok. Stir in a mixture of salt, pepper, lemon juice, and soy sauce. Heat thoroughly.
2. Add green beans and toss with sauce. Turn into a heated serving dish.

About 6 servings

Old-fashioned Green Beans

¾ pound fresh green beans
8 slices bacon, diced
2 medium potatoes, pared and
    cut into ½-inch pieces
1 small onion, sliced
¼ cup water
½ teaspoon salt

1. Cut green beans into 1-inch pieces. Cook in boiling salted water until tender; drain.
2. Fry bacon in a wok until crisp. Stir in green beans, potatoes, onion, water, and salt.
3. Cook, covered, over medium heat about 15 minutes, or until potatoes are tender.

About 4 servings

Fried Green Pepper Strips

2 large green peppers
½ cup fine dry bread crumbs
⅓ cup grated Parmesan cheese
1½ teaspoons salt
⅛ teaspoon pepper
1 egg, fork beaten
2 tablespoons water
    Oil for frying

1. Clean green peppers and cut into ⅛-inch rings. Cut each ring into halves or thirds.
2. Coat with a mixture of bread crumbs, cheese, salt, and pepper. Dip into a mixture of egg and water. Coat again with crumb mixture. Chill 1 hour.
3. Heat a 1-inch layer of oil to 375°F in a large wok. Cover surface with chilled green pepper strips. Fry about 30 seconds, or until golden brown. Remove strips with fork or slotted spoon. Drain on absorbent paper.

4 servings

Mushrooms à la Crème

½ pound fresh mushrooms
1 teaspoon butter
1 teaspoon dry sherry or
    Madeira
½ cup dairy sour cream
    Salt and pepper

1. Remove stems from mushrooms and chop; leave caps whole. Sauté the mushrooms in butter in cooking pan of a chafing dish 2 minutes. Add sherry and cook 1 minute.
2. Add sour cream and season to taste. Place over simmering water and heat thoroughly (do not boil).
3. Serve on **toast points**.

2 servings

Mushrooms Supreme

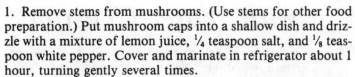

2 pounds mushrooms
3 tablespoons lemon juice
¼ teaspoon salt
⅛ teaspoon white pepper
½ cup butter or margarine
2 tablespoons grated onion
¼ teaspoon Worcestershire
   sauce
¼ teaspoon salt
¼ teaspoon white pepper
   Few grains cayenne pepper
¼ cup shredded sharp Cheddar
   cheese

1. Remove stems from mushrooms. (Use stems for other food preparation.) Put mushroom caps into a shallow dish and drizzle with a mixture of lemon juice, ¼ teaspoon salt, and ⅛ teaspoon white pepper. Cover and marinate in refrigerator about 1 hour, turning gently several times.
2. Remove mushrooms from marinade and drain thoroughly on absorbent paper. Heat half the butter in cooking pan of a chafing dish over direct heat. Add about half the mushroom caps and half the grated onion.
3. Cook 10 to 15 minutes, or until caps are lightly browned and tender, turning with a spoon occasionally. Remove mushroom caps to a bowl and cook remaining mushrooms.
4. Place all mushroom caps in cooking pan and add Worcestershire sauce, salt, white pepper, and cayenne pepper. Toss gently to mix.
5. Sprinkle cheese over mushrooms and set pan over simmering water to keep hot while serving. Serve mushrooms on **toast triangles** and garnish with **parsley sprigs.**

6 to 8 servings

Mushrooms in Sour Cream

1½ pounds fresh mushrooms
½ cup butter
½ large clove garlic, chopped
1 small onion, sliced
¼ teaspoon paprika
2 tablespoons white wine
½ cup dairy sour cream

1. Wash mushrooms and pat dry. Slice lengthwise through caps and stems.
2. Heat butter in a large wok. Add garlic and onion; cook until onion is soft.
3. Add mushrooms and paprika; stir-fry mushrooms about 5 minutes, or until mushrooms are lightly browned.
4. Add wine to wok, reduce heat, and cook mushrooms several minutes, stirring occasionally.
5. Just before serving, blend in sour cream and heat about 1 minute. Serve immediately on **hot fluffy rice.**

4 to 6 servings

Sesame Hashed Brown Potatoes

¼ cup butter
1 tablespoon minced green onion
¼ cup sesame seed
4 large baking potatoes, pared
   and cut into small cubes
1 teaspoon salt
⅛ teaspoon white pepper
6 tablespoons whipping cream
2 teaspoons chopped parsley

1. Melt butter in cooking pan of a chafing dish over chafing dish burner. Stir in green onion and continue cooking until softened.
2. Stir in sesame seed and continue cooking until lightly browned, stirring occasionally.
3. Add potatoes to cooking pan. Sprinkle with salt and pepper. Stir in whipping cream.
4. Cook over chafing dish burner until potatoes are golden brown, stirring occasionally. Sprinkle with parsley and serve.

4 to 6 servings

Parsnip Fritters

1   **pound parsnips (about 4), scrubbed and pared**
2   **eggs, well beaten**
1   **tablespoon butter or margarine**
½   **cup milk**
1   **teaspoon minced onion**
3   **tablespoons flour**
¼   **teaspoon dill weed**
¾   **teaspoon salt**
     Few grains pepper
     Oil for deep frying

1. Cook parsnips in boiling salted water until tender; drain thoroughly.
2. Mash the parsnips, removing any fibrous portions. (There will be about 1¼ cups mashed.)
3. Add eggs to parsnips; beat well. Beat in butter, milk, onion, and a mixture of flour, dill weed, salt, and pepper until thoroughly blended.
4. Slowly heat oil in a wok to 365°F.
5. Drop batter by tablespoonfuls into hot oil and fry 2 to 3 minutes, turning several times until fritters are golden brown. Remove with slotted spoon, drain over oil, and place on absorbent paper.
6. Serve hot.

About 4 servings

Stir-Fried Peas

1   **package (10 ounces) frozen peas, thawed**
1   **tablespoon vegetable oil**
½   **teaspoon salt**
⅛   **teaspoon pepper**
1   **medium onion, peeled, cut in half lengthwise, and sliced ¼ inch thick**

1. Drain peas on paper toweling to remove as much moisture as possible.
2. Heat oil in a large wok. Stir in salt and pepper. Add drained peas; stir-fry to coat with oil and heat through. Simmer, covered, over medium heat 2 minutes.
3. Stir in onion and continue cooking 2 minutes.
4. Serve immediately.

4 servings

Summer Squash with Dill

2   **pounds (about 4 small) summer squash (yellow straight-neck), washed**
½   **cup boiling water**
2   **teaspoons finely chopped fresh dill**
½   **teaspoon salt**
1   **cup dairy sour cream**
1   **tablespoon lemon juice**
2   **teaspoons sugar**
½   **teaspoon paprika**

1. Trim ends from squash and cut squash into thin, crosswise slices. Put into a large saucepan with water, dill, and salt. Cover and simmer 15 minutes, or until just tender; drain.
2. Meanwhile, thoroughly heat remaining ingredients in cooking pan of a chafing dish over boiling water, stir constantly.
3. Add squash to sauce and toss gently.

About 6 servings

Creamed Spinach with Almonds

1 tablespoon flour
¾ teaspoon salt
⅛ teaspoon ground nutmeg
1 tablespoon butter or margarine
1 cup cream
2 tablespoons toasted almond
  halves
1 package (10 ounces) frozen
  spinach, cooked and drained

1. Blend flour, salt, and nutmeg into hot butter in cooking pan of a chafing dish. Heat until bubbly. Gradually add cream, stirring constantly. Bring to boiling; stir and cook 1 to 2 minutes.
2. Add almonds and spinach to sauce; mix lightly to blend. Serve garnished with **tomato wedges.**

About 4 servings

Caramel Sweet Potatoes

⅓ cup butter
½ cup walnut pieces
1 cup firmly packed brown sugar
½ teaspoon salt
½ cup orange juice
6 medium (about 2 pounds) sweet
  potatoes, cooked
⅓ cup brandy

1. Melt butter in cooking pan of a chafing dish. Stir in walnut pieces. Cook over moderate heat until lightly toasted.
2. Remove walnuts from pan. Add brown sugar, salt, and orange juice to butter remaining in cooking pan; stir to blend. Bring to boiling and boil 3 to 4 minutes, stirring occasionally.
3. Peel the sweet potatoes and cut in halves lengthwise. Add to the syrup with walnut pieces.
4. Place cooking pan over chafing dish burner. Heat the potatoes gently, basting with the syrup. Warm the brandy, pour over potatoes, and ignite. Serve when flames die out.

6 servings

Summer Squash with Bacon

2 pounds (about 4 small)
  summer squash (yellow
  straight-neck), washed
3 slices bacon, diced
¼ cup finely chopped onion
1 teaspoon salt
  Few grains pepper

1. Trim ends from squash and cut squash into thin diagonal slices; set aside.
2. Cook bacon in a wok until crisp and brown. Remove bacon from wok and all but 3 tablespoons of the bacon drippings.
3. Stir in squash, onion, salt, and pepper. Cover and cook over medium heat 12 minutes, or until squash is tender. Stir in bacon and serve.

About 6 servings

Creole Fried Tomatoes

1 small clove garlic, minced
1 tablespoon finely chopped
  parsley
½ teaspoon salt
  Dash pepper
¼ cup finely chopped onion
1 tablespoon olive oil
2 large tomatoes, cut into
  ½-inch-thick slices
2 tablespoons cornmeal
2 teaspoons olive oil

1. Combine garlic, parsley, salt, pepper, and onion. Mix in 1 tablespoon olive oil.
2. Spread both sides of each tomato slice with mixture. Sprinkle slices with cornmeal.
3. Heat 2 teaspoons olive oil in a large wok. Fry tomato slices until lightly browned, pushing slices up sides as they are cooked. (Additional oil may be added, if necessary.)

4 servings

Mallow Sweet Potato Balls

3 cups warm mashed sweet
    potatoes
  Salt and pepper to taste
3 tablespoons melted butter
8 large marshmallows
1 egg
1 tablespoon cold water
1 cup almonds, blanched and.
    chopped
  Oil for deep frying

1. Season potatoes and add butter. Mold potato mixture around marshmallows, forming 8 balls with a marshmallow in center of each.
2. Beat egg and mix with cold water. Dip sweet potato balls in egg and then in almonds.
3. Slowly heat oil in a wok to 365°F. When oil is hot, fry sweet potato balls until brown, turning occasionally.

8 servings

Deep-Fried Zucchini

1¼ cups all-purpose flour
1 teaspoon salt
¼ teaspoon pepper
2 eggs, well beaten
¾ cup milk
1 teaspoon Worcestershire sauce
1 tablespoon butter or margarine,
    melted
  Oil for deep frying
6 medium (about 2 pounds)
    zucchini, cut in halves cross-
    wise and into ¾-inch sticks
    lengthwise

1. Blend flour, salt, and pepper in a bowl. Add a mixture of eggs, milk, Worcestershire sauce, and butter; beat just until smooth.
2. Heat oil in a fondue pot to 365°F.
3. Dip zucchini sticks into batter, using a fork to coat evenly. Allow any excess coating to drip off.
4. Fry 2 to 3 minutes, or until golden brown. Lift from oil and drain a few seconds before removing to absorbent paper.
5. Sprinkle with **salt.**

6 servings

Zucchini Parmesan

2 tablespoons cooking oil
1 small clove garlic, minced
4 medium zucchini, thinly sliced
⅓ cup coarsely chopped onion
1 tablespoon chopped parsley
1 teaspoon salt
⅛ teaspoon pepper
¼ teaspoon oregano
¼ teaspoon rosemary
2 cups chopped peeled tomatoes
¼ cup grated Parmesan cheese

1. Heat oil in a large wok. Add garlic and stir-fry about 1 minute. Stir in zucchini, onion, and parsley. Sprinkle with a mixture of salt, pepper, oregano, and rosemary. Stir together and cover.
2. Heat about 5 minutes over medium heat. Stir in tomatoes and cook, uncovered, 1 to 2 minutes, or until tomatoes are thoroughly heated.
3. Turn mixture into a serving dish and sprinkle with cheese.

4 or 5 servings

DESSERTS AND BEVERAGES

Banana Split Fondue

2   king-size chocolate crunch
    candy bars (about 6½
    ounces each)
1   cup milk
    Ripe bananas, cut into bite-
    size pieces
    Large marshmallows
    Maraschino cherries with
    stems

1. Break candy bars into pieces over fondue saucepan. Pour milk over candy-bar pieces.
2. Place saucepan over low heat just long enough to warm mixture. Stir occasionally until chocolate melts. If mixture becomes too thick for dipping, stir in 1 to 2 tablespoons milk.
3. Spear banana pieces and marshmallows; dip in melted chocolate. Cherries may be held by the stems for dipping.

4 to 6 servings

Chocolate Fondue

4   ounces (4 squares) unsweetened
    chocolate
1   eup sugar
½   cup whipping cream
5   tablespoons butter or margarine
2   tablespoons orange liqueur
½   teaspoon vanilla extract
    Assorted dippers (marshmallows,
    strawberries with hulls, apple
    slices, banana chunks,
    mandarin orange segments,
    cake cubes)

1. Cut up chocolate and melt in fondue pot over low heat. Stir in sugar, whipping cream, and butter.
2. Cook over low heat until thickened (about 5 minutes), stirring constantly. Stir in orange liqueur and vanilla extract.
3. Place over very low heat to keep warm while dipping.

4 servings

Eggnog Fondue

2   eggs, beaten
2   tablespoons sugar or honey
⅛   teaspoon salt
1½ cups milk
½   teaspoon vanilla extract
3   tablespoons arrowroot
3   tablespoons dark rum
    Nutmeg
    Fruitcake, cut into ¾-inch
    pieces

1. Beat together eggs, sugar, and salt. Stir in milk and vanilla extract.
2. Pour eggnog into a nonmetal fondue pot. Mix arrowroot with 1 tablespoon rum and stir into the eggnog.
3. Cook over medium heat until mixture thickens, stirring occasionally. Stir in remaining rum.
4. Keep fondue warm while dipping fruitcake pieces.

6 to 8 servings

Orange Chocolate Fondue

2 packages (3¼ ounces each)
  chocolate pudding and pie
  filling
3 cups orange juice
1 cup milk
2 tablespoons butter or margarine
  Marshmallows
  Pound cake cubes
  Ladyfingers, cut in thirds
  Maraschino cherries with stems
  Walnut halves

1. In a large saucepan, mix together pudding, orange juice, and milk. Cook over low heat, stirring constantly, until mixture thickens and comes to boiling. Remove from heat.
2. Stir in butter until melted. Pour mixture into a fondue pot. Serve with marshmallows, cake cubes, ladyfingers, cherries, and walnuts.

8 servings

Glazed Fruit in Chafing Dish

2 tart red apples, cored
2 tablespoons lemon juice
2 tablespoons butter
3 tablespoons brown sugar
1 large banana
½ cup pineapple chunks, fresh
  or unsweetened canned
1 cup pineapple juice
1 tablespoon cornstarch
  Vanilla ice cream

1. Cut apples into wedges. Dip in lemon juice and place in medium-size bowl.
2. Melt butter in cooking pan of a chafing dish over medium heat. Toss apple slices with half the brown sugar and stir into melted butter. Cover and cook over medium heat 7 to 8 minutes, stirring occasionally.
3. When apple slices are almost tender, slice banana into chunks and add with pineapple to apple mixture. Sprinkle remaining brown sugar over fruit, cover, and cook several minutes until bananas are glazed.
4. Remove fruit from cooking pan. Stir in pineapple juice mixed with cornstarch. Simmer a few minutes, stirring occasionally, until sauce thickens.
5. Return fruit to sauce, warm, and serve over ice cream.

4 servings

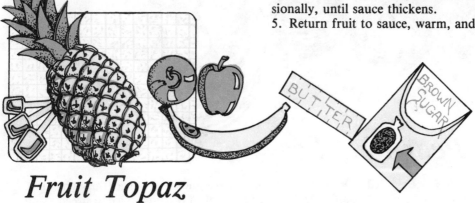

Fruit Topaz

3 apples, pared, cored, and sliced
3 pears, pared, cored, and sliced
1 cup firmly packed light brown
  sugar
1 tablespoon nutmeg
1 cup golden raisins
½ cup slivered almonds
¼ cup butter or margarine
¼ cup lemon-lime carbonated
  beverage

1. Place apple and pear slices in cooking pan of a chafing dish. Combine sugar and nutmeg and sprinkle over fruit.
2. Sprinkle raisins and almonds over fruit. Dot top of mixture with butter. Pour carbonated beverage over all.
3. Cook over medium heat until fruit is tender (15 to 20 minutes).
4. Keep warm over simmering water while serving.

6 servings

Brandied Bananas

4 large green-tipped bananas,
    sliced diagonally into 1-inch
    pieces
3 tablespoons lime juice
¼ cup butter or margarine
½ cup sugar
½ cup apricot brandy
1 cup dairy sour cream or yogurt
    Brown sugar

1. Sprinkle bananas with lime juice. Heat butter in cooking pan of a chafing dish over medium flame of chafing dish burner.
2. Add bananas and heat quickly. Stir in sugar and all but 2 tablespoons apricot brandy. Heat remaining brandy in a ladle or a large serving spoon. Ignite the warm brandy and pour over the bananas. Shake the pan gently or stir until flame dies down.
3. Serve the bananas topped with dairy sour cream and a sprinkling of brown sugar.

4 servings

Peach Flambée Ambrosia

1 tablespoon butter
¼ cup slivered almonds
2 tablespoons light brown sugar
2 tablespoons orange juice
1 package (16 ounces) frozen
    sliced peaches, thawed
    Vanilla ice cream
¼ cup shredded coconut
¼ cup Grand Marnier

1. Heat butter in cooking pan of a chafing dish over low heat. Add almonds and brown lightly. Stir in brown sugar and orange juice. Add peaches and heat.
2. Place scoops of vanilla ice cream in dessert dishes and sprinkle with coconut.
3. Warm liqueur in a ladle. Ignite and pour over the peaches. Shake the pan gently or stir until flames die out. Spoon over ice cream.

4 to 6 servings

Strawberry-Pear Flambée

2 packages (10 ounces each) frozen
    strawberries
1 cup sugar
6 tablespoons butter
½ cup orange juice
1½ teaspoons grated lemon peel
1 can (29 ounces) large pear halves,
    drained
⅓ cup cognac

1. Drain strawberries; reserve juice. Put berries through a sieve to purée. Add desired amount of reserved juice to sweeten and thin purée; set aside.
2. In cooking pan of a chafing dish, caramelize sugar with butter over medium heat. Stir in orange juice, lemon peel, and purée. Simmer sauce 1 to 2 minutes, stirring gently.
3. Place pears in sauce and roll in sauce until they are thoroughly heated and have a blush.
4. In a separate pan, heat cognac just until warm. Ignite the cognac and pour over the pears. Spoon the sauce over pears until the flames die out.
5. Serve the pears in dessert dishes with the sauce.

4 servings

Crepes Suzette

Crepes:
- **1 cup all-purpose flour**
- **1 teaspoon sugar**
- **1 pinch salt**
- **1 egg, well beaten**
- **1 cup milk**
- **2 tablespoons butter**

Sauce:
- **½ cup sugar**
- **Peelings (white portion removed) and juices of 1 orange and ½ lemon**
- **¼ cup butter**
- **1 ounce Grand Marnier**
- **1 ounce cognac**
- **1 ounce Cointreau**

1. To prepare crepes, mix all ingredients except butter in a bowl; beat until smooth (batter should be the consistency of thin cream).
2. Put a small amount of butter in an 8-inch skillet; heat until the butter bubbles. Pour in enough batter to form a 6-inch circle, quickly rotating the pan to spread the batter thinly and evenly. Cook over medium heat about ½ minute; turn crepe and cook other side.
3. With the aid of a fork and a spoon, carefully fold the crepe in fourths. Transfer to a heated plate and keep warm. Repeat process until all the batter is used.
4. To prepare sauce, heat ¼ cup of the sugar in cooking pan of a chafing dish over low heat, stirring until sugar is caramelized. Add the citrus peelings and the butter; stir until butter is melted.
5. Add the citrus juices; cook and stir several minutes. Remove the peelings from the sauce.
6. To serve, transfer folded crepes to the sauce. Sprinkle the remaining sugar over crepes. Add the liqueurs to sauce and ignite.
7. Serve 3 crepes per person on hot dessert plates.

4 servings

Emperor's Dessert
(Kaiserschmarren)

- **2 tablespoons butter**
- **1 cup all-purpose flour**
- **¼ cup sugar**
- **¼ teaspoon salt**
- **3 eggs, beaten**
- **1 cup milk**
- **¾ cup butter**
- **¾ cup sugar**
- **½ teaspoon ground cinnamon**
- **½ cup golden raisins, plumped**
- **½ cup flaked or sliced almonds, toasted**

1. Melt 2 tablespoons butter in a heavy 6-inch skillet and set aside.
2. Combine flour, ¼ cup sugar, and salt in a bowl. Add a mixture of eggs, milk, and melted butter. Beat until smooth.
3. Heat skillet to moderately hot. Pour in just enough batter to cover bottom. Immediately tilt skillet to spread batter thinly and evenly.
4. Cook each crepe over medium heat until light brown on bottom and firm to touch on top. Turn and brown other side. As each crepe is cooked, transfer to a hot platter.
5. Using two forks, gently tear the crepes into 1-inch irregular-shaped pieces; set aside and keep warm.
6. Melt ¾ cup butter in cooking pan of a chafing dish; stir in ¾ cup sugar. Mix in cinnamon, raisins, and almonds, stirring occasionally until heated.
7. Add crepe pieces and toss lightly to coat.

8 to 10 servings

Glazed Whole Oranges

4 large navel oranges
3 tablespoons butter
¾ cup currant jelly
½ cup orange juice
1 tablespoon arrowroot
2 tablespoons cold water

1. Remove thin outer peel from three of the oranges with a vegetable peeler. Cut into very thin slivers and place in a small saucepan with enough water to cover. Cover saucepan.
2. Bring to boiling, reduce heat, and simmer 10 minutes. Drain and set peel aside. Cut remaining peel and white membrane from all four oranges.
3. Put butter and jelly in cooking pan of a chafing dish. Place over low heat and stir gently until melted. Stir in orange juice and cooked peel, reserving some to garnish oranges, if desired.
4. Place oranges in sauce. Cook about 5 minutes; spoon sauce over oranges occasionally. Mix arrowroot with cold water to form a smooth paste; stir into sauce.
5. Continue cooking until sauce thickens (about 5 minutes); spoon sauce over oranges while heating.
6. Serve oranges warm, covered with sauce, and sprinkle with reserved slivered peel, if desired.

6 to 8 servings

Fried Cream

⅓ cup sugar
¼ cup cornstarch
¼ teaspoon salt
4 egg yolks
¼ cup milk
2 cups whipping cream, scalded
½ teaspoon vanilla extract
Fine dry bread crumbs
2 eggs, slightly beaten
Oil for deep frying

1. Mix sugar, cornstarch, and salt in a heavy saucepan.
2. Mix egg yolks with milk; blend with dry ingredients. Add scalded cream, stirring until smooth.
3. Cook and stir mixture until thickened and smooth.
4. Remove from heat and stir in vanilla extract. Turn into a lightly greased 8-inch square dish or pan. Chill thoroughly.
5. Cut cream into squares. Coat with bread crumbs, then with slightly beaten eggs, and again with bread crumbs.
6. Pour oil into wok, filling wok not more than a third full. Heat to 365°F. Fry cream squares in hot oil until browned (about 2 minutes).

25 pieces

Golden Tea Punch

3 cups hot strong tea
3 tablespoons sugar
3 cups orange juice
½ cup pineapple juice
½ cup Galliano
1 stick cinnamon

1. Combine all ingredients in cooking pan of a chafing dish.
2. Bring to boiling and simmer, uncovered, 5 minutes. Float **orange slices** or garnish with **fresh mint**. Keep punch warm over chafing dish burner.

About 8 servings

INDEX